Mermaids Adult Coloring Book Vol 3

60 Entertaining Stress Relieving Mermaid Patterns

By Omar Johnson

I0499717

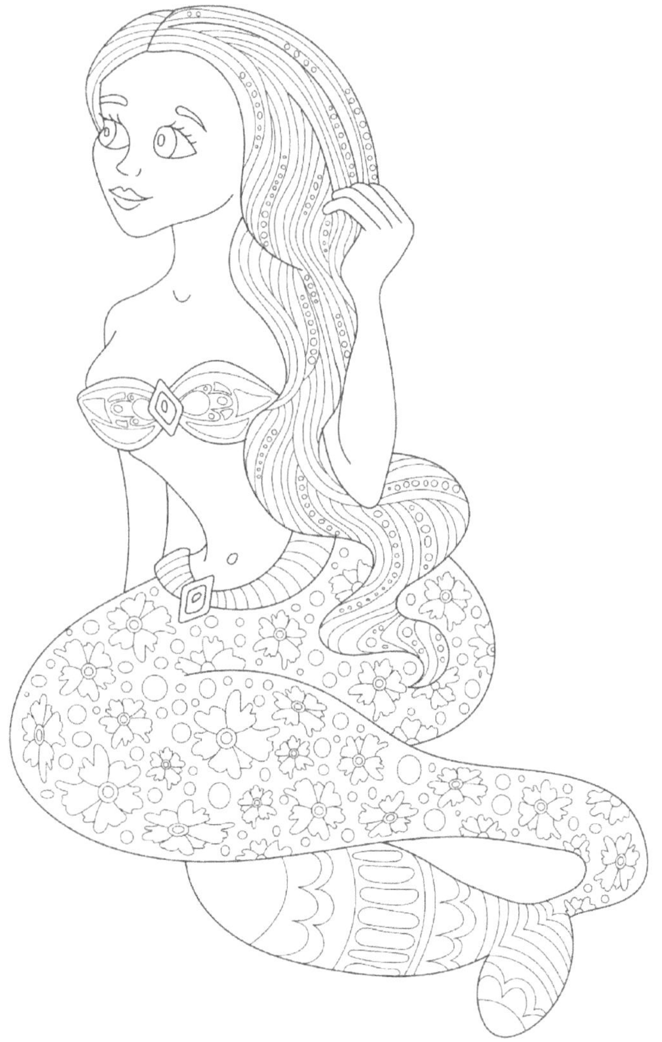

Get Your Free Butterfly Mandala Coloring Book

Visit

HTTPS://WWW.ADULTCOLORINGBOOKSFORYOU.COM

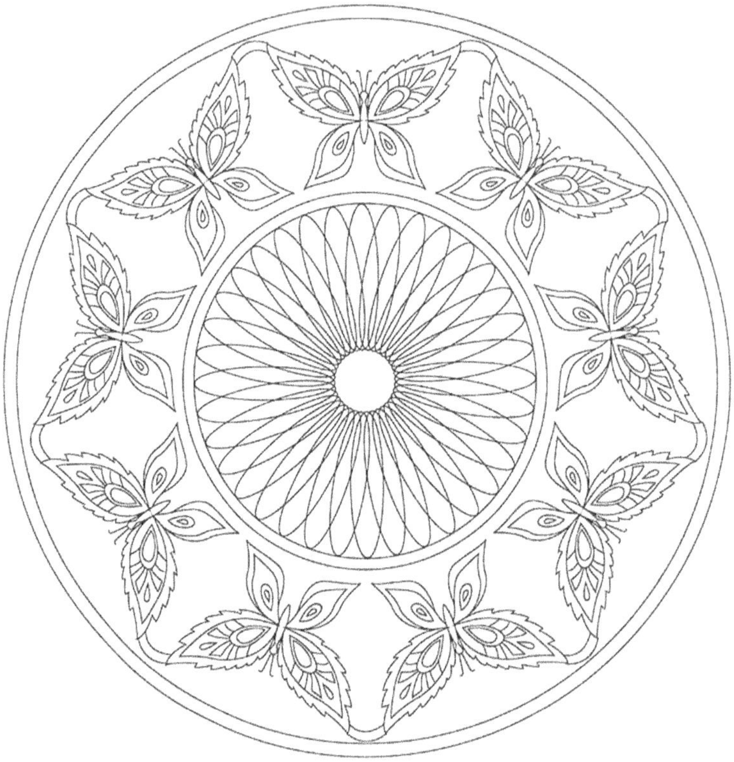

Make Profits Easy LLC Publishing

omarjohnson@adultcoloringbooksforyou.com

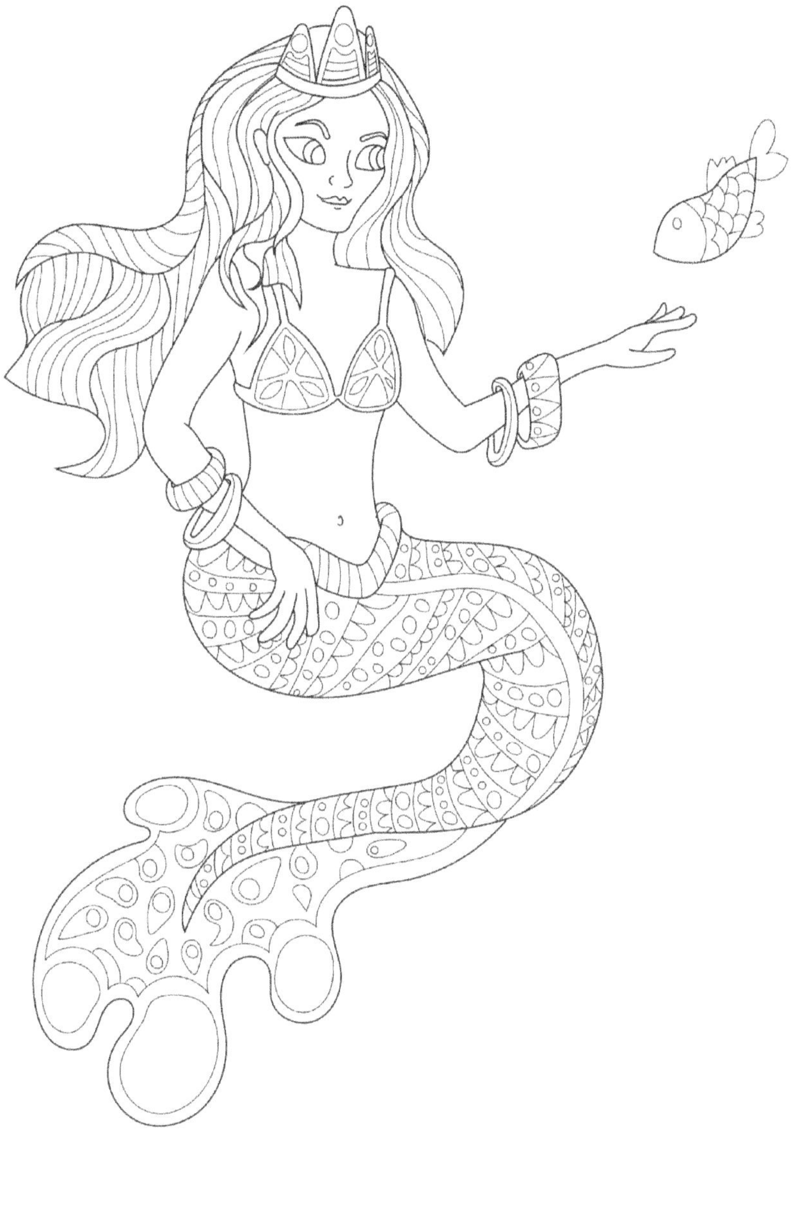

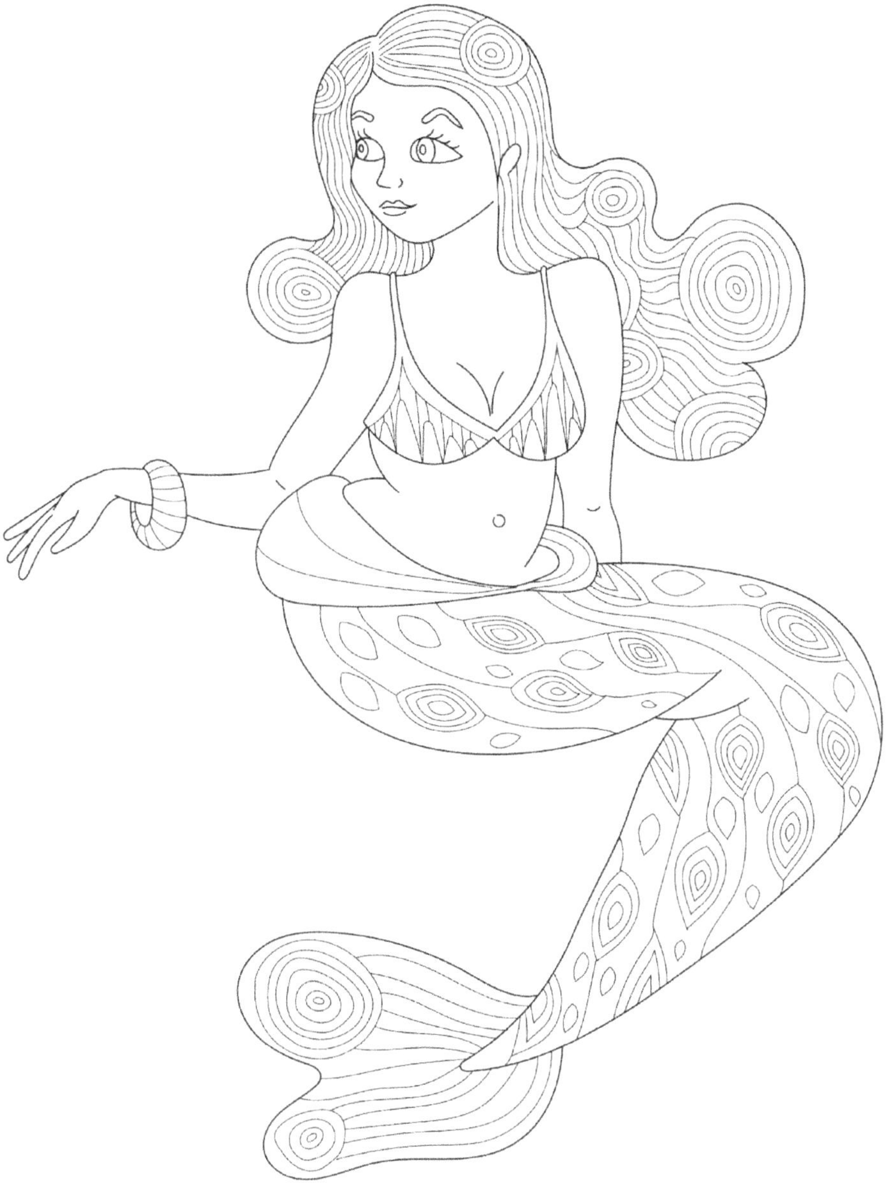

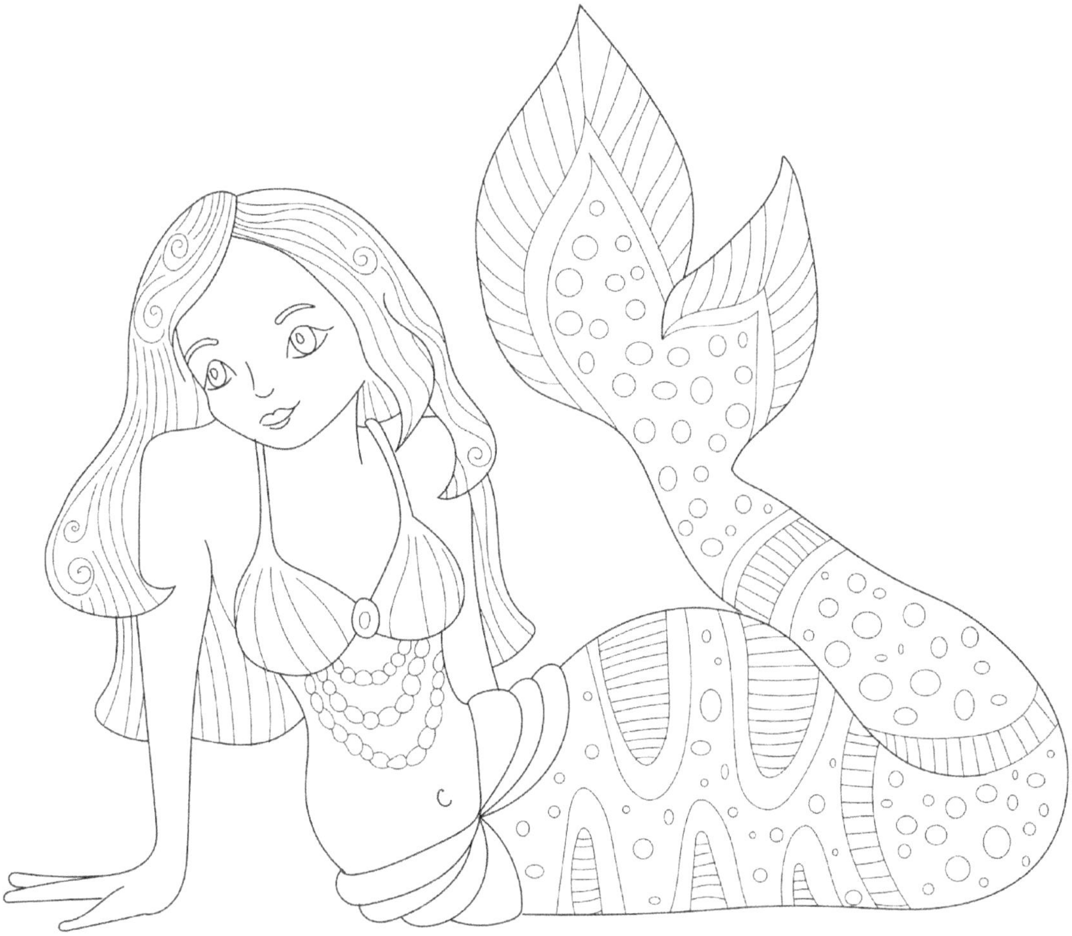

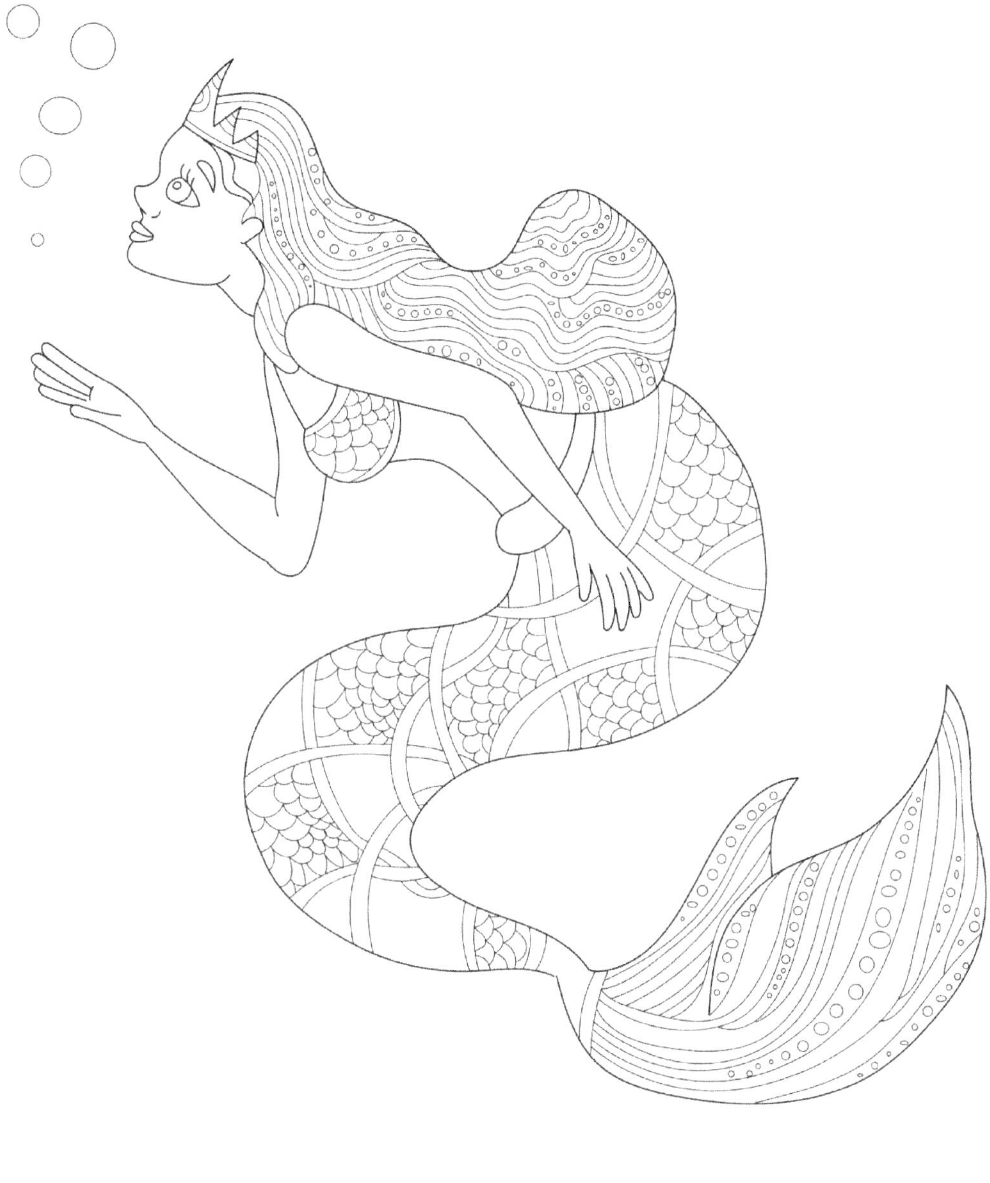

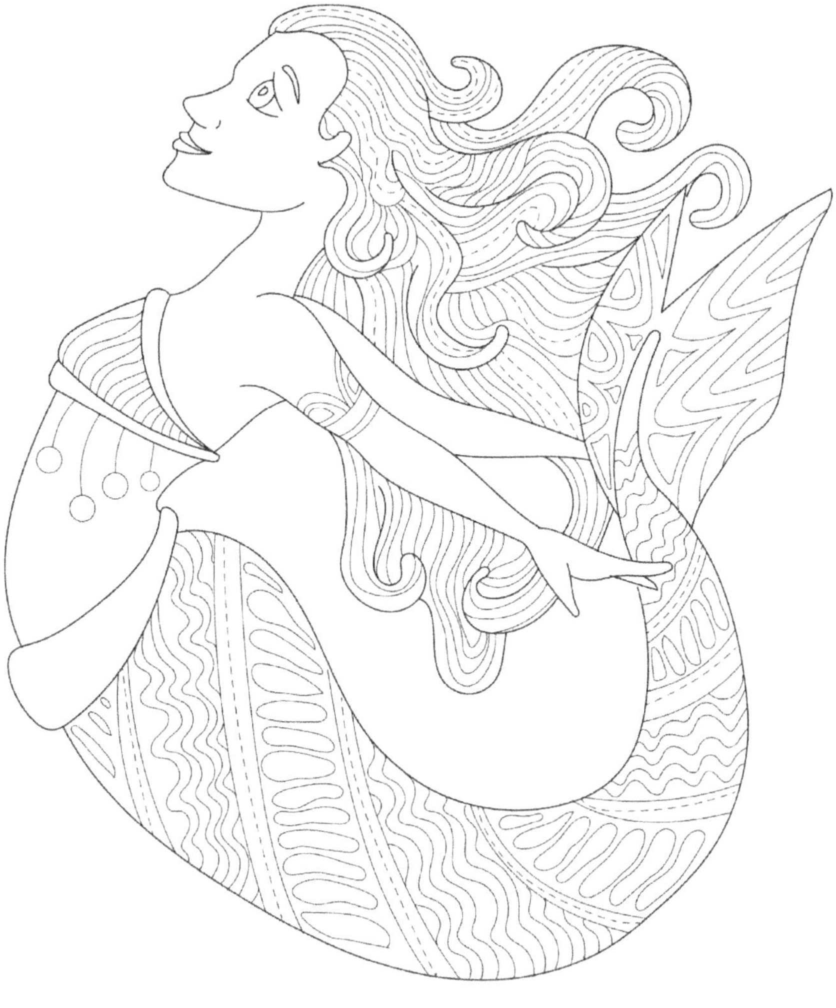

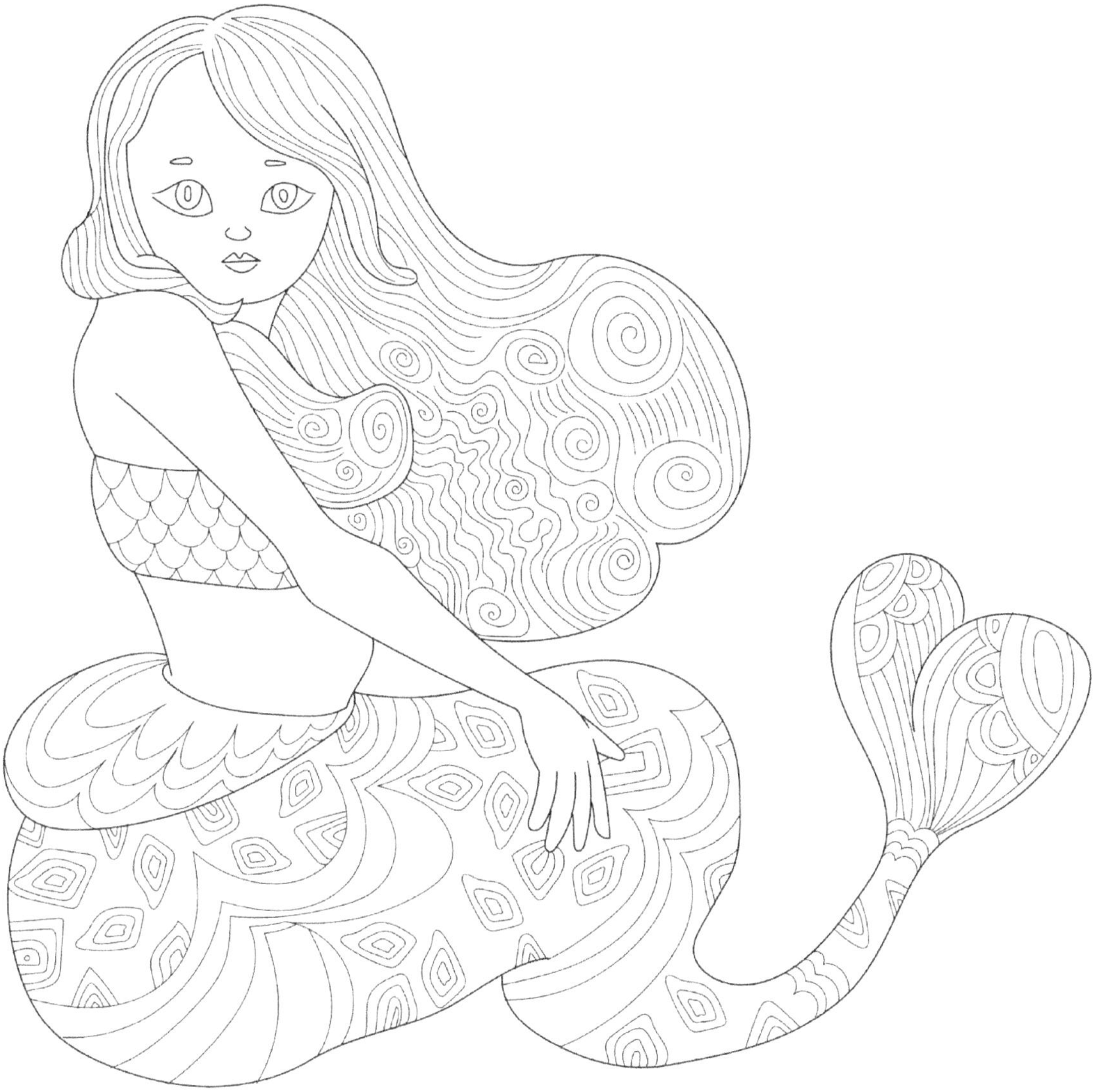

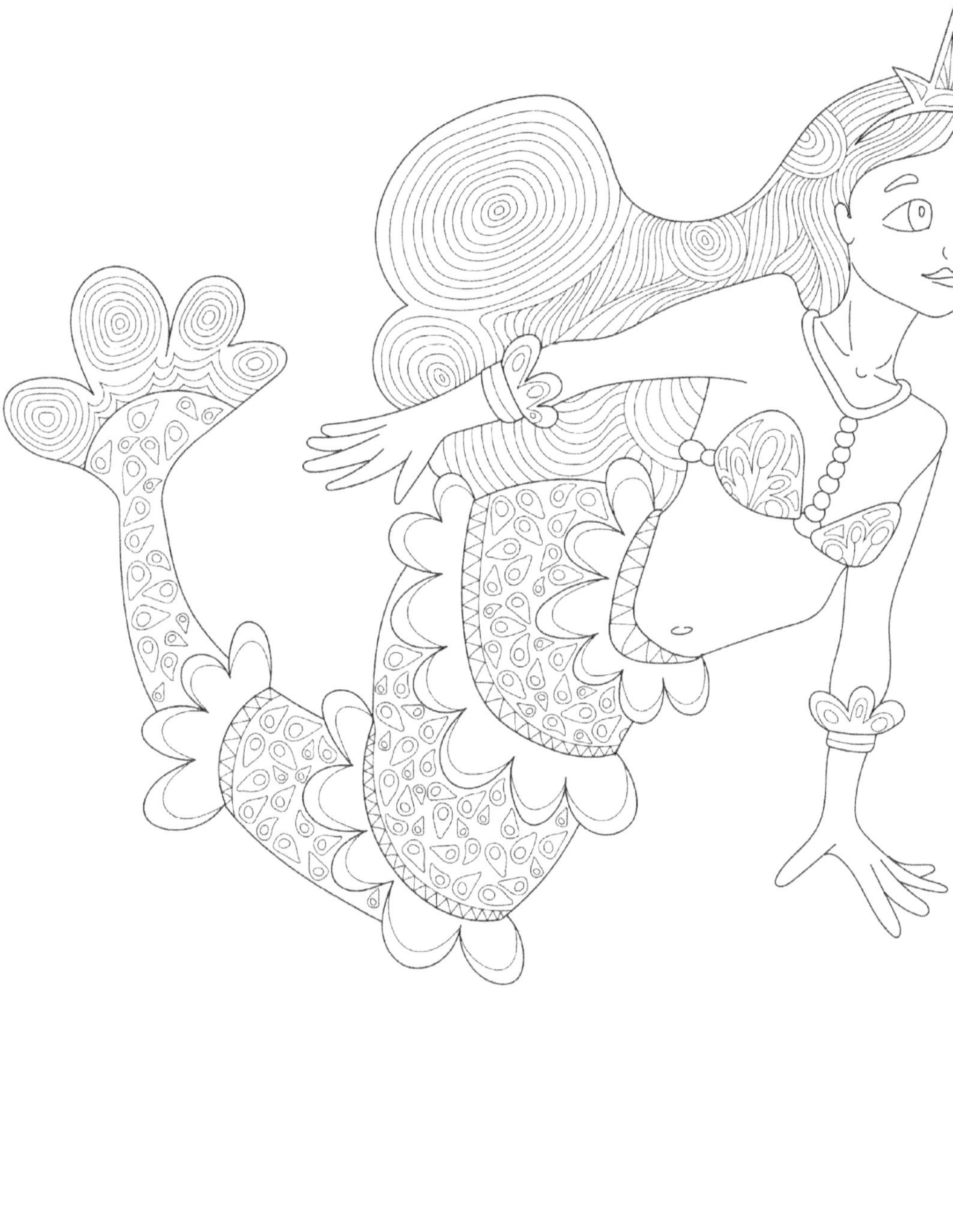

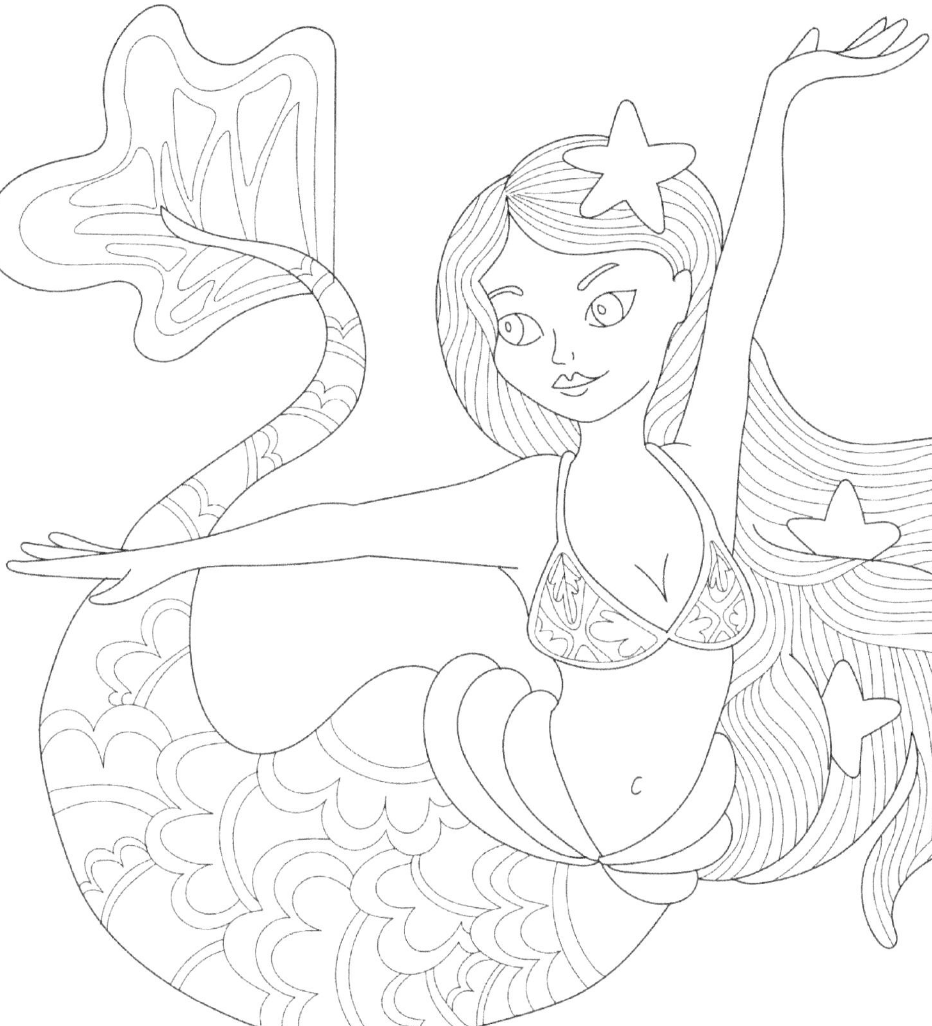

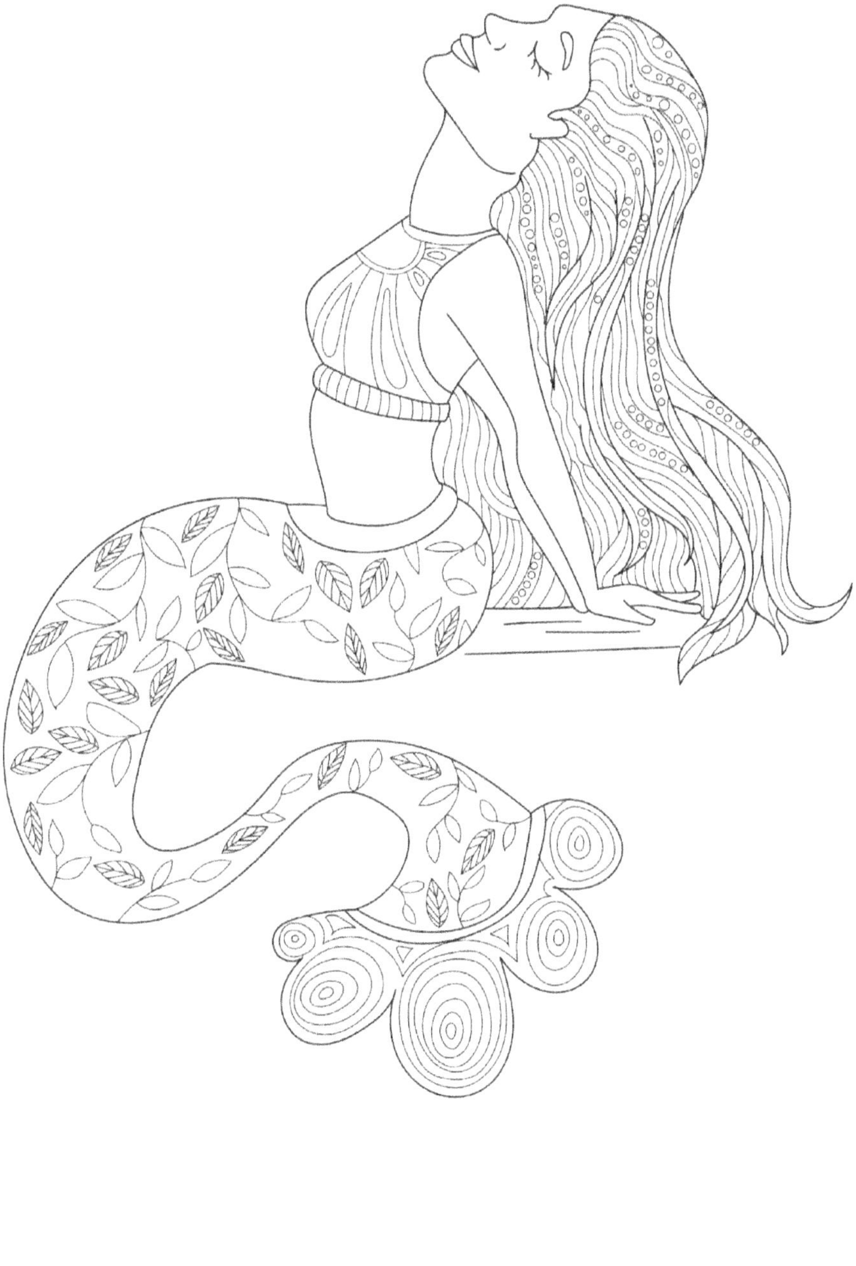

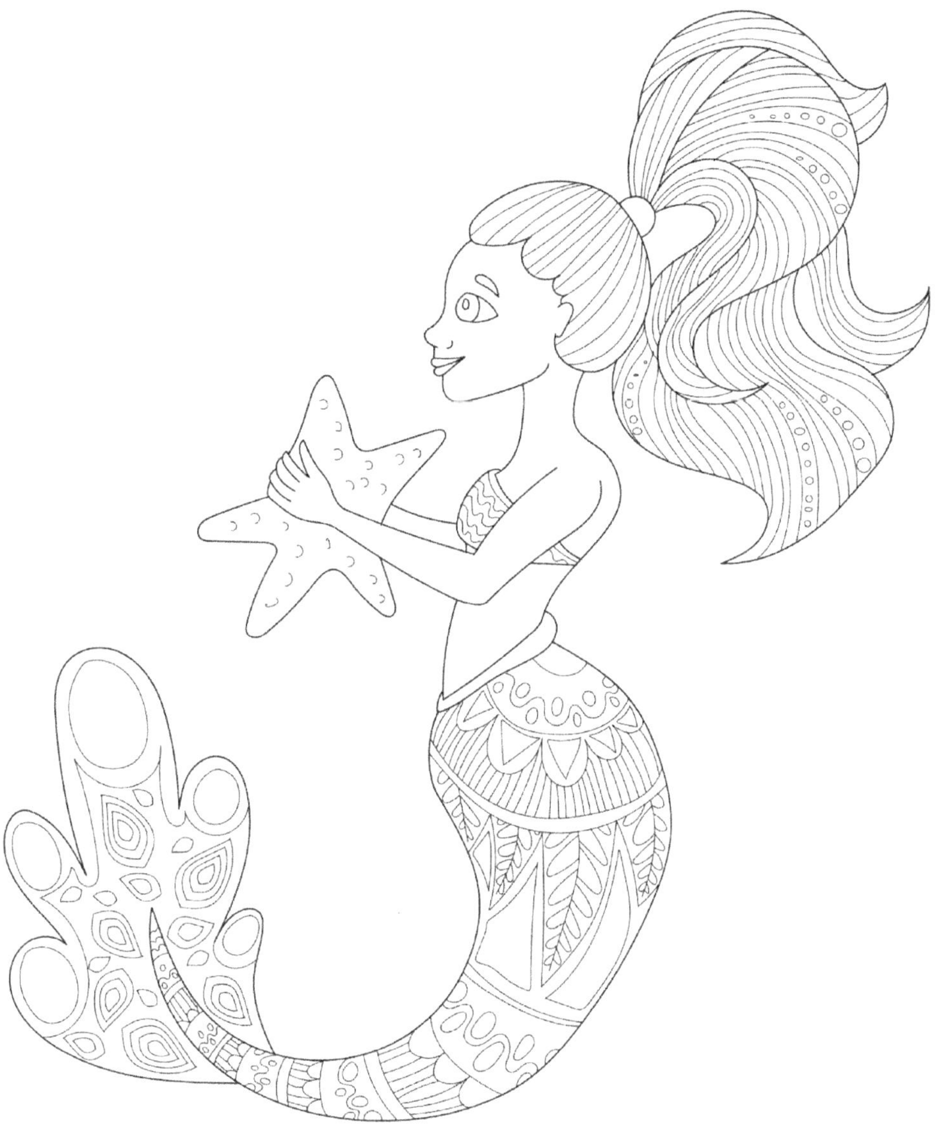

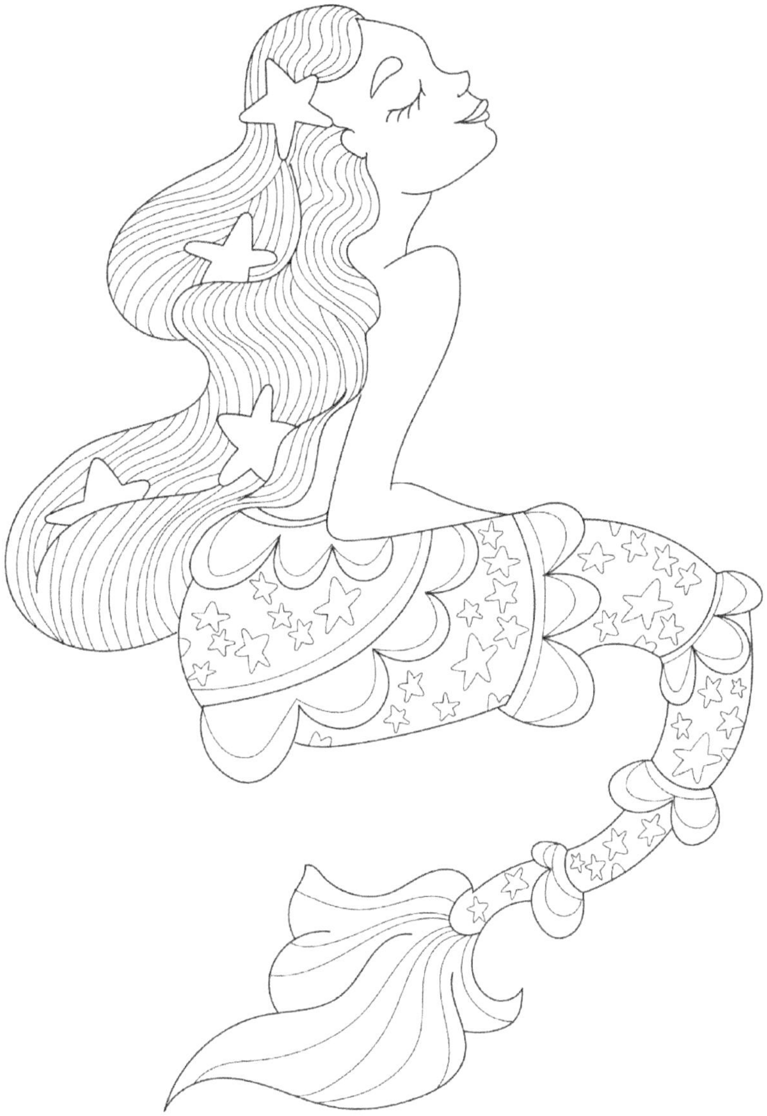

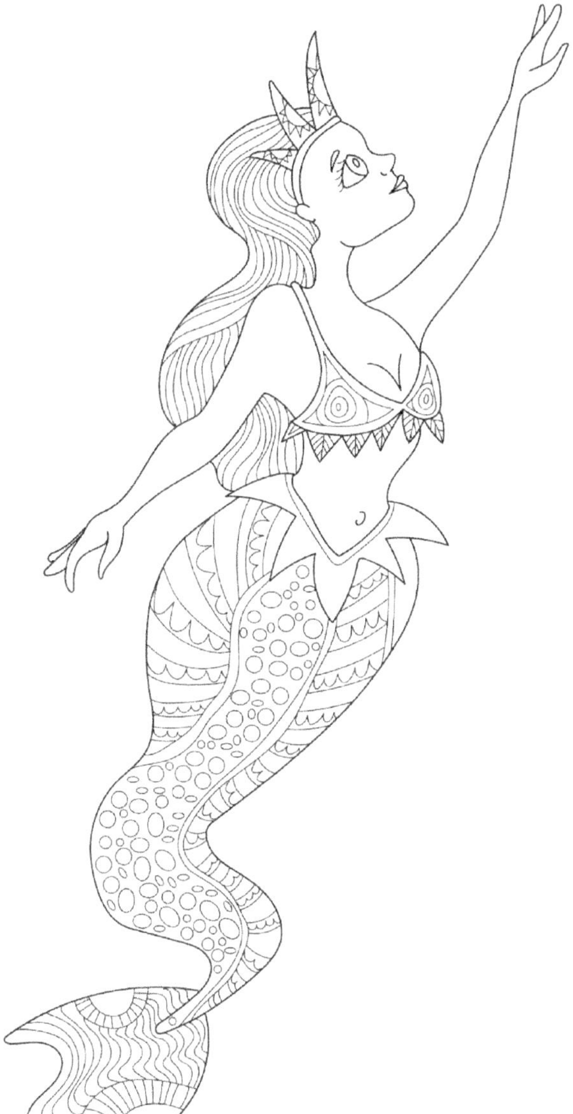

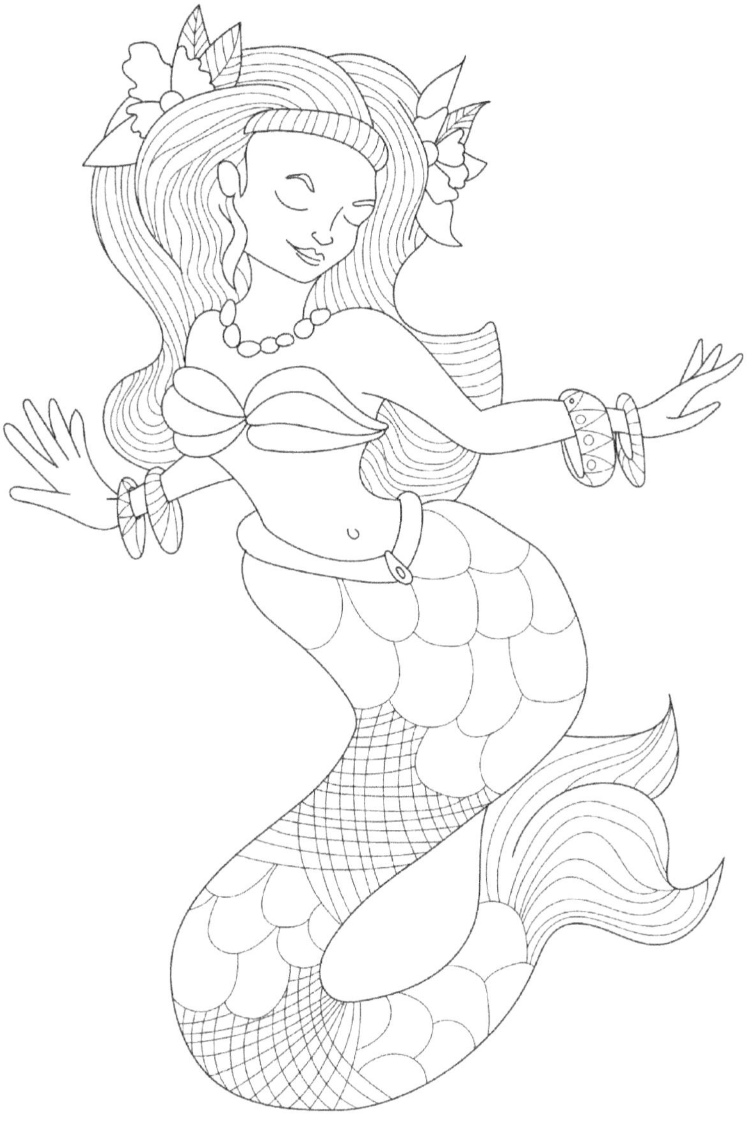

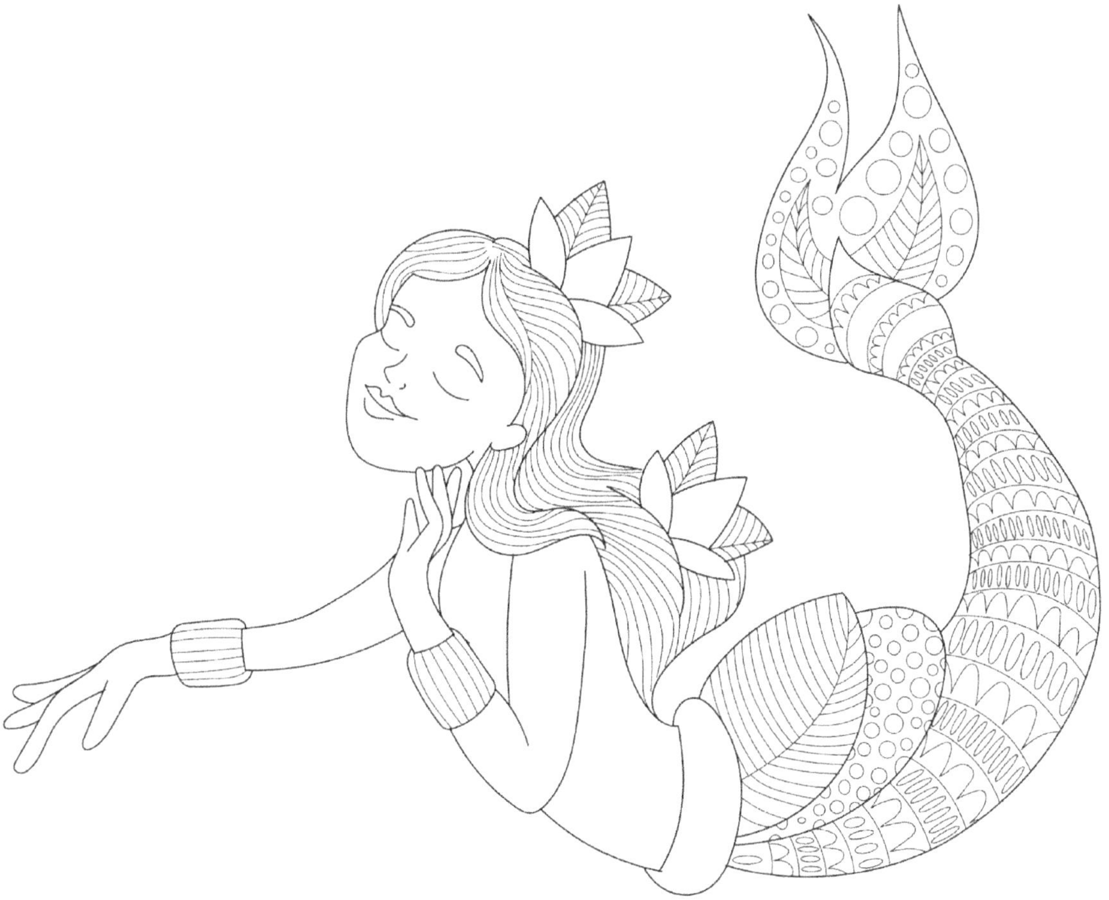

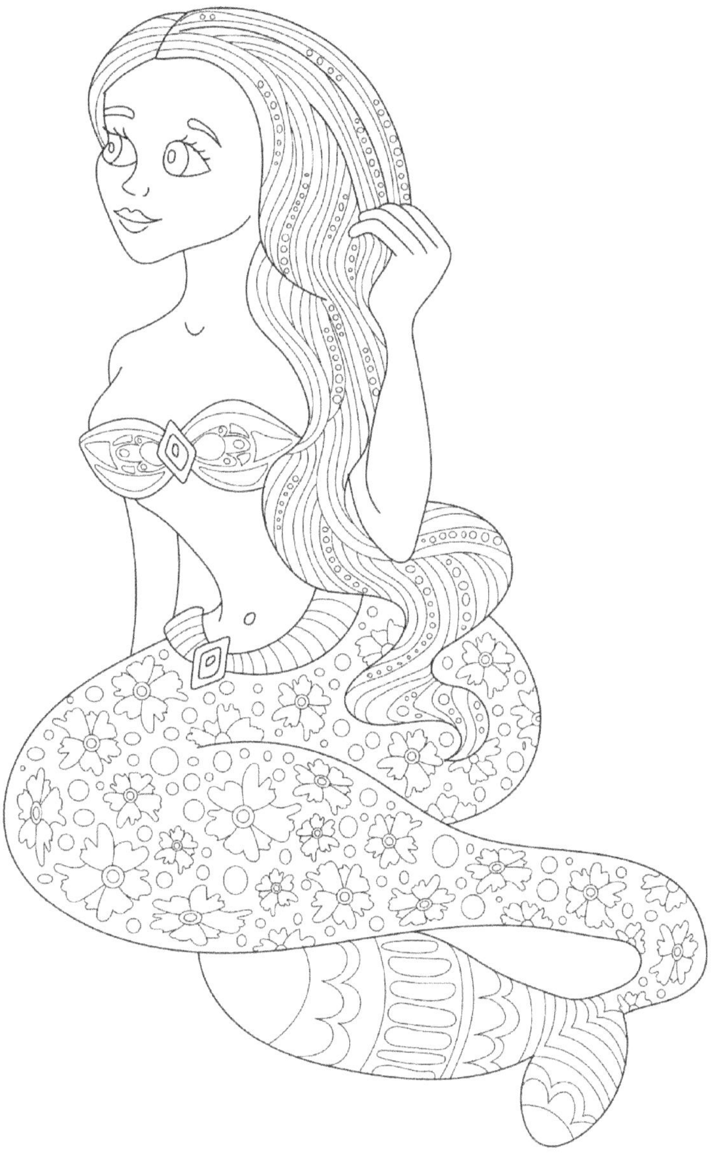

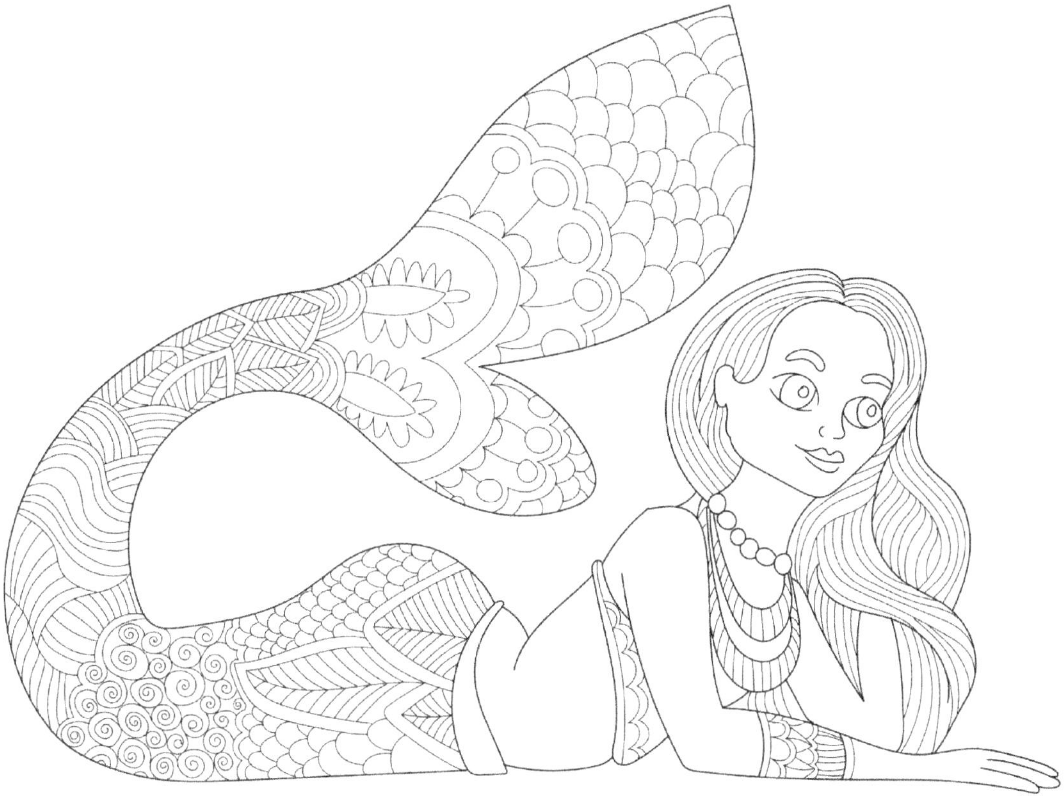

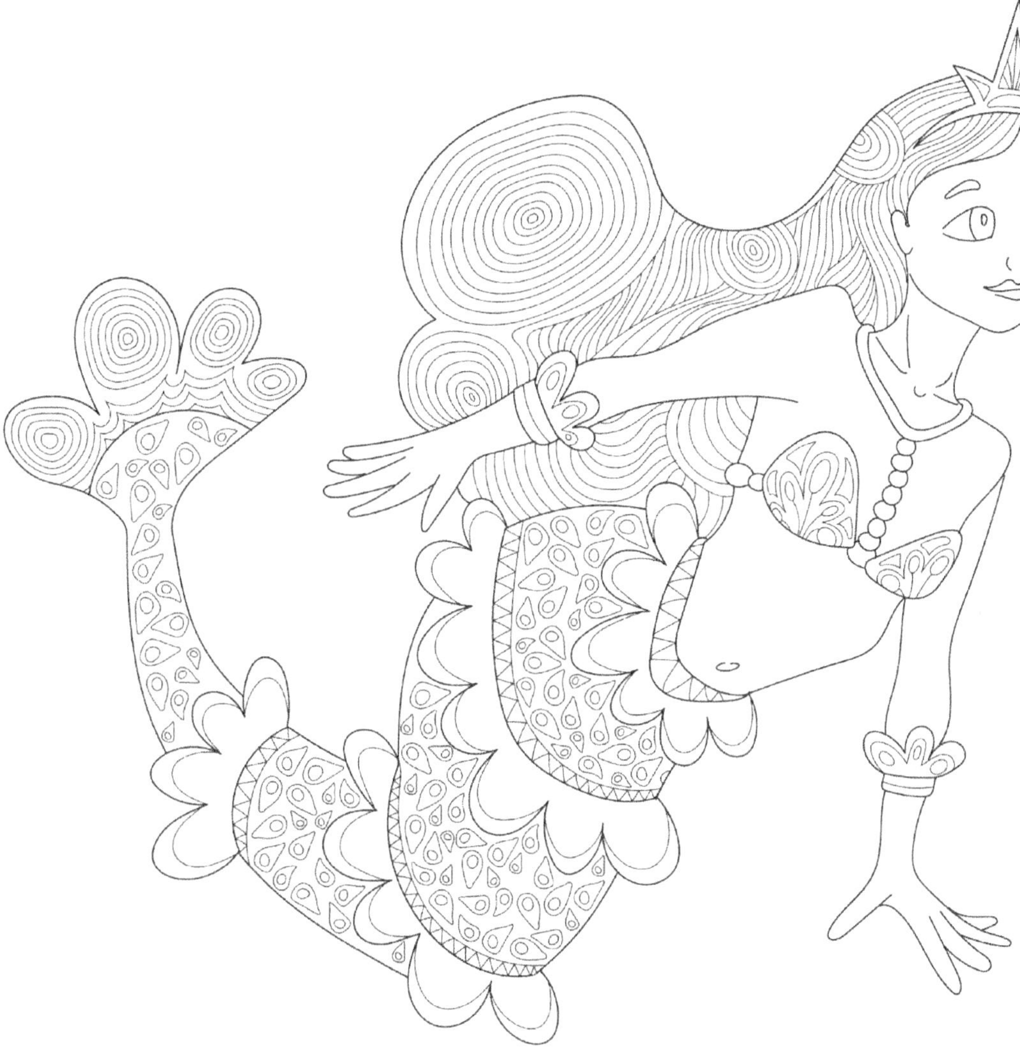

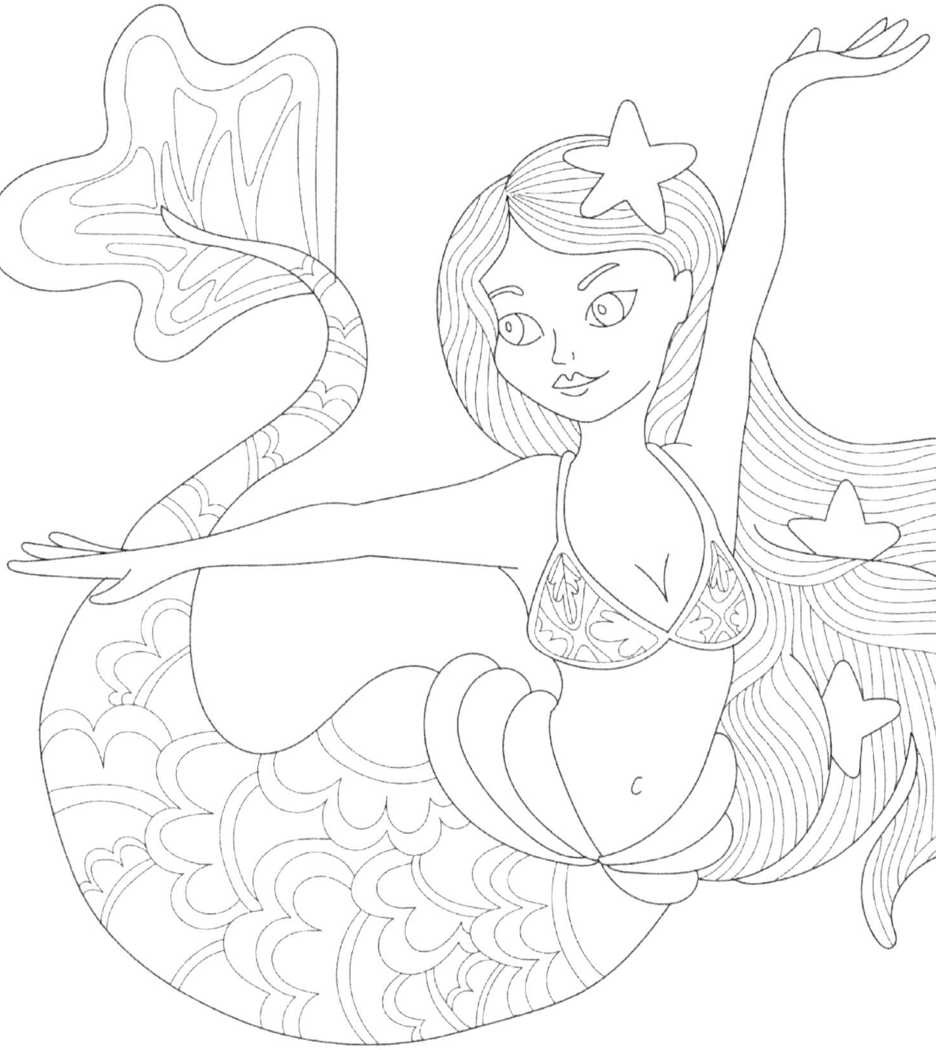

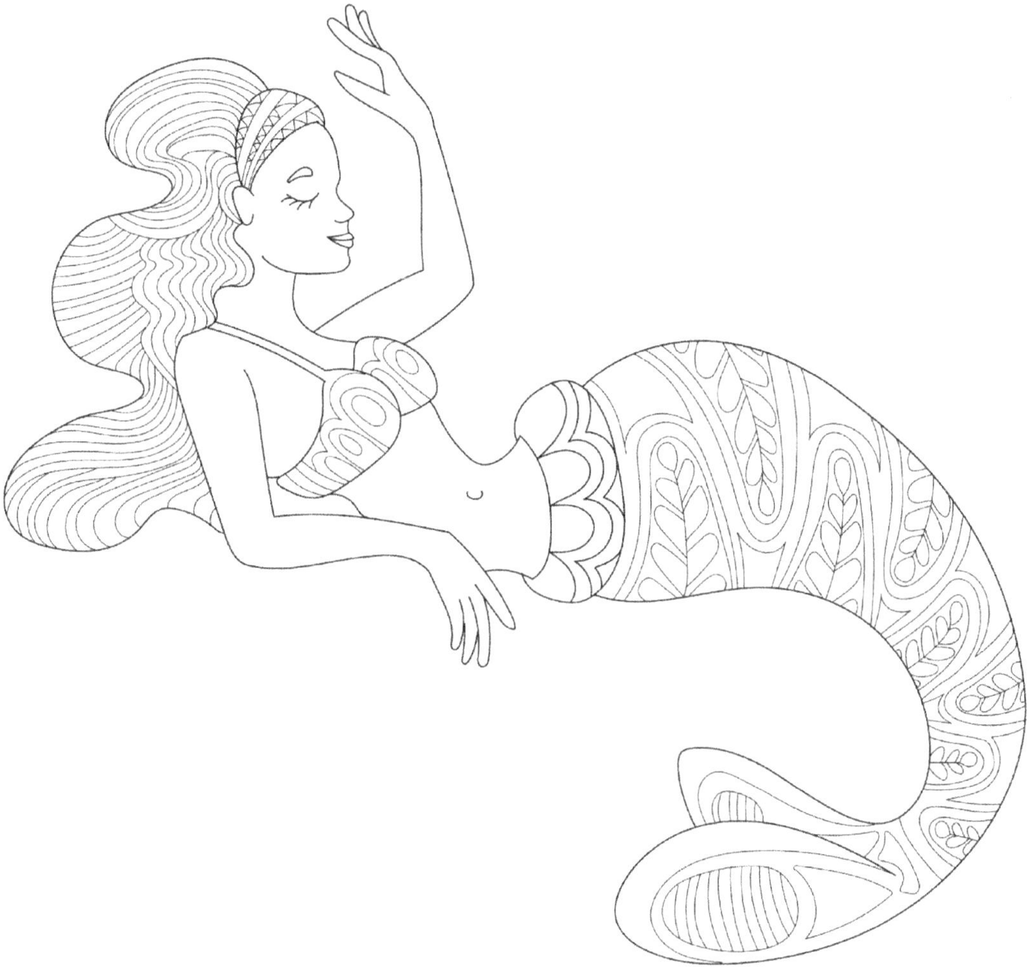

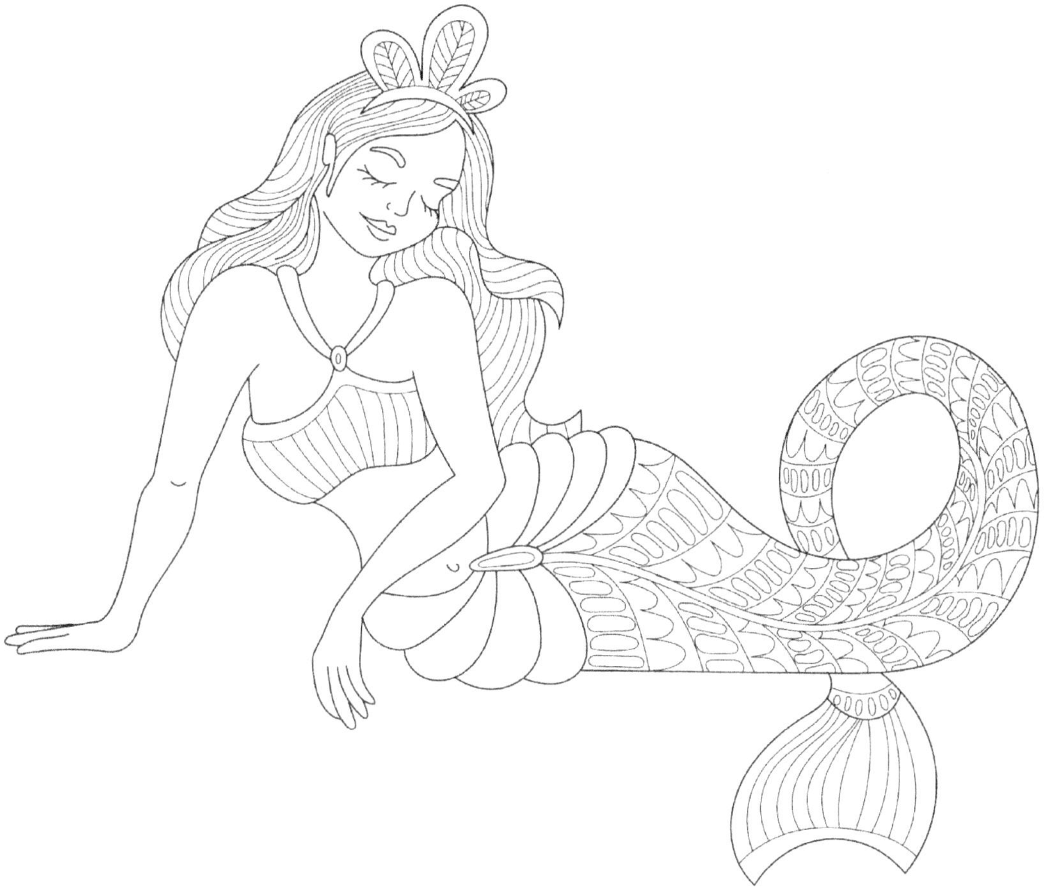

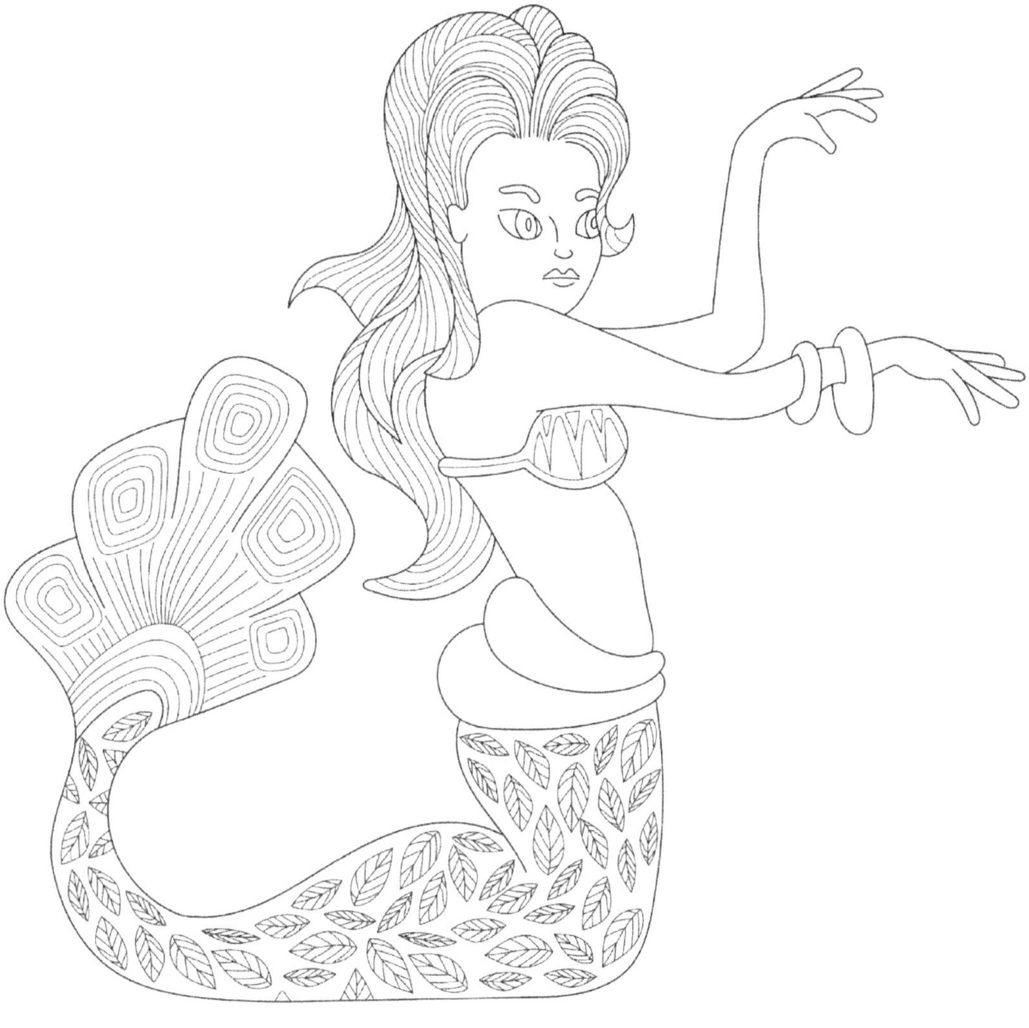

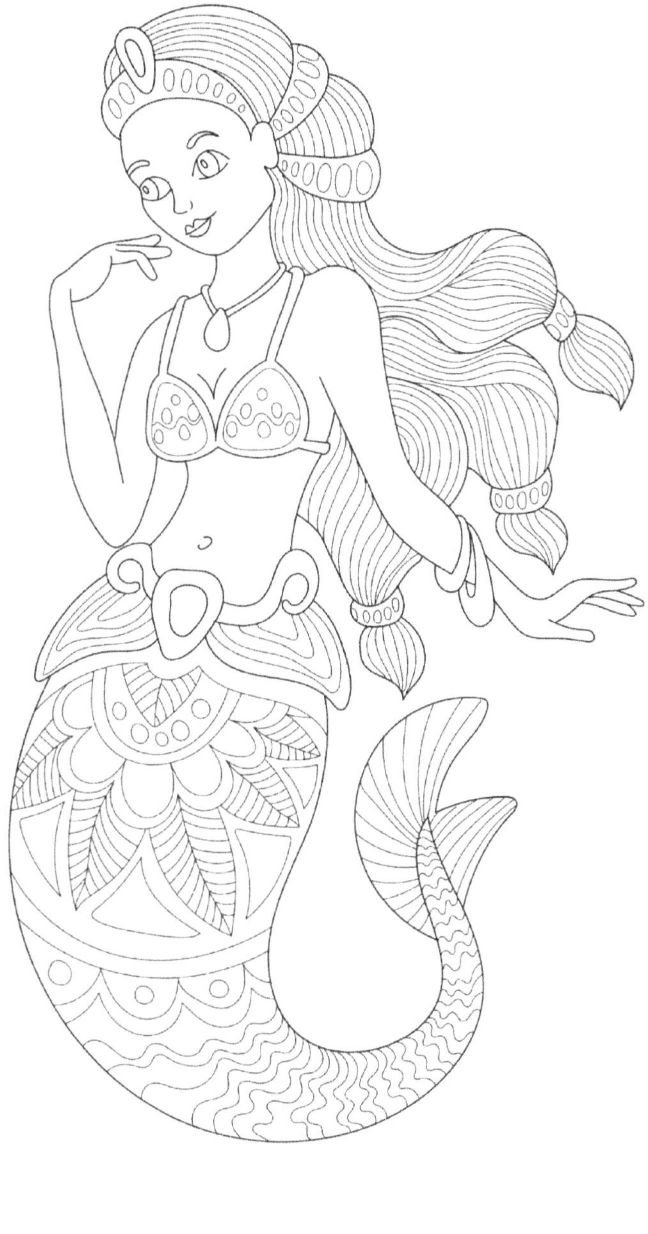

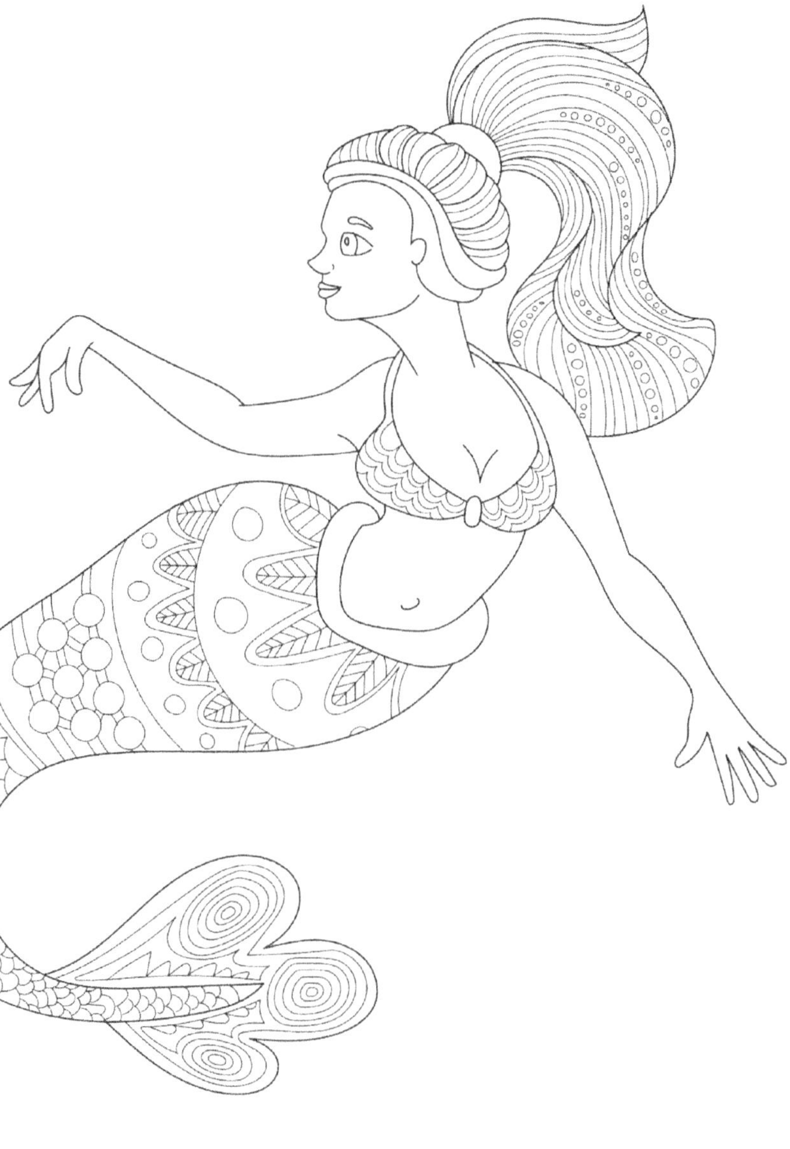

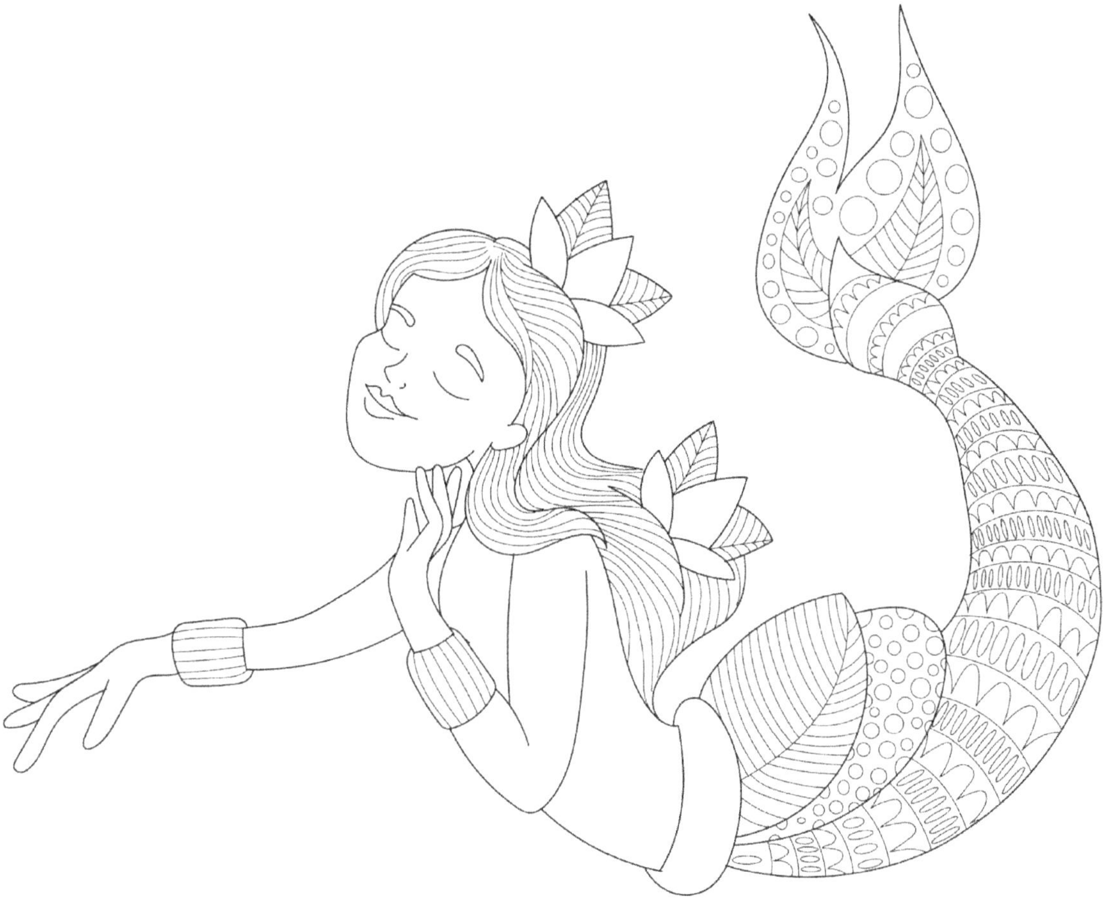

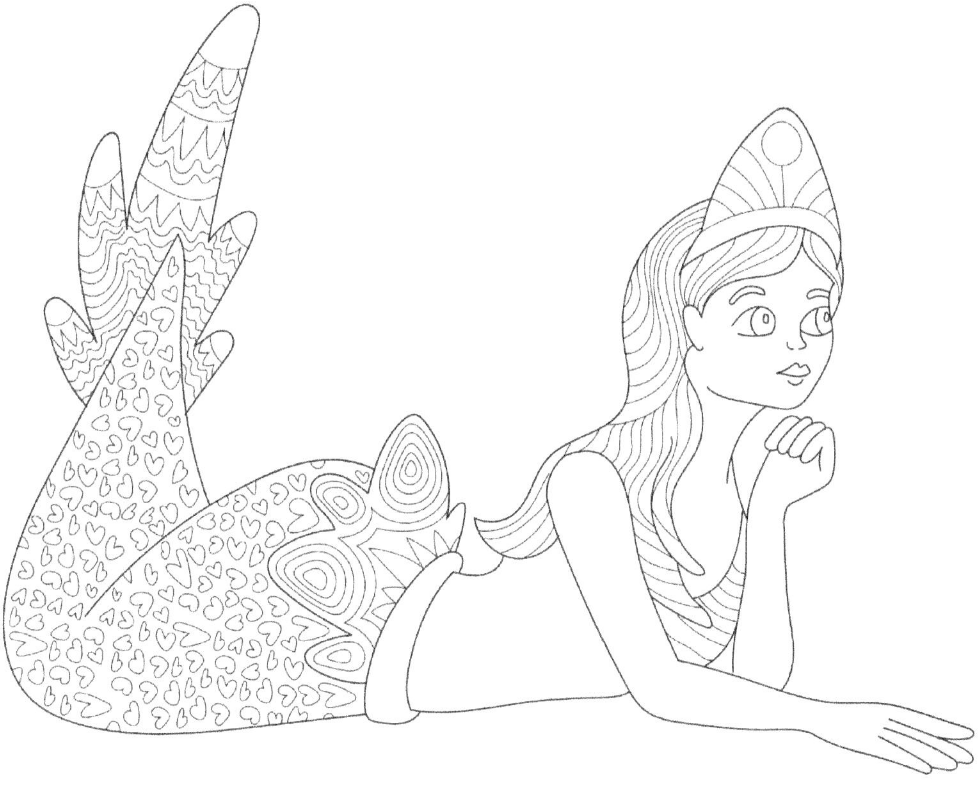

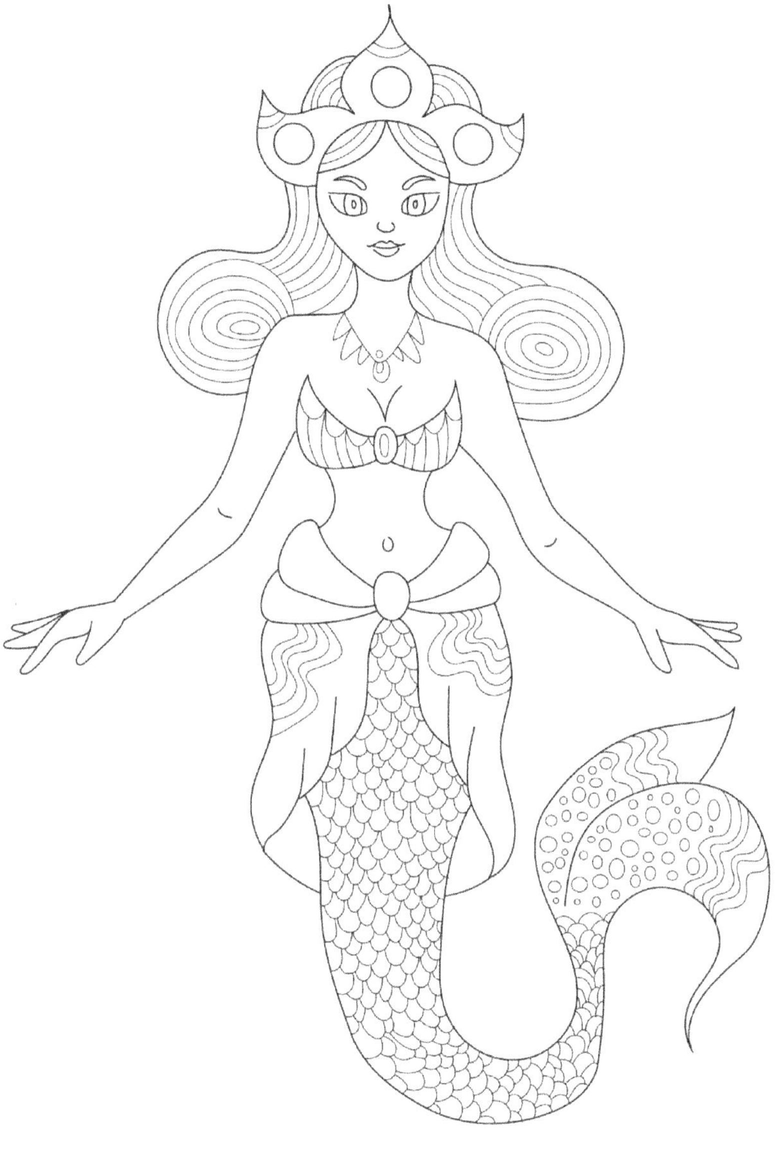

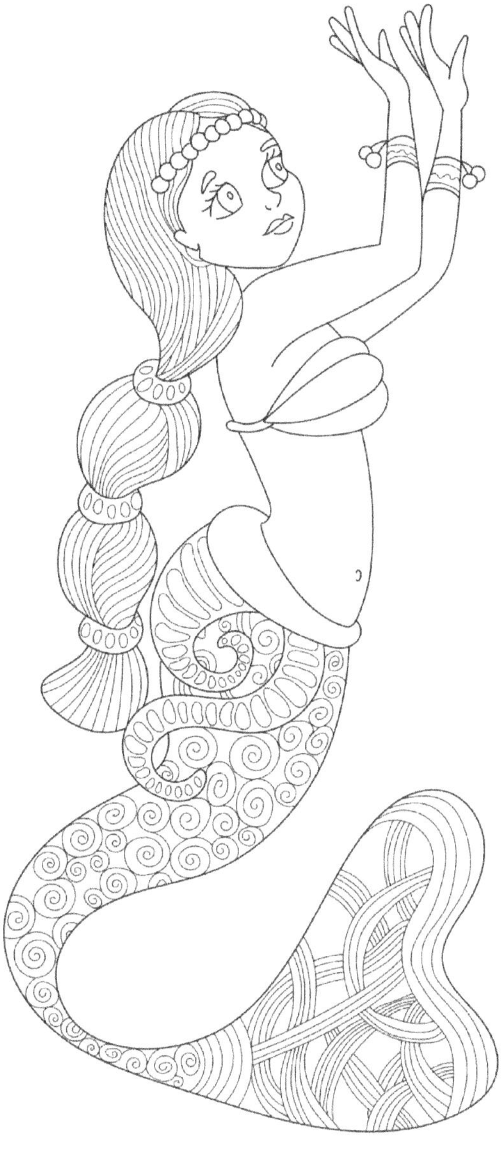

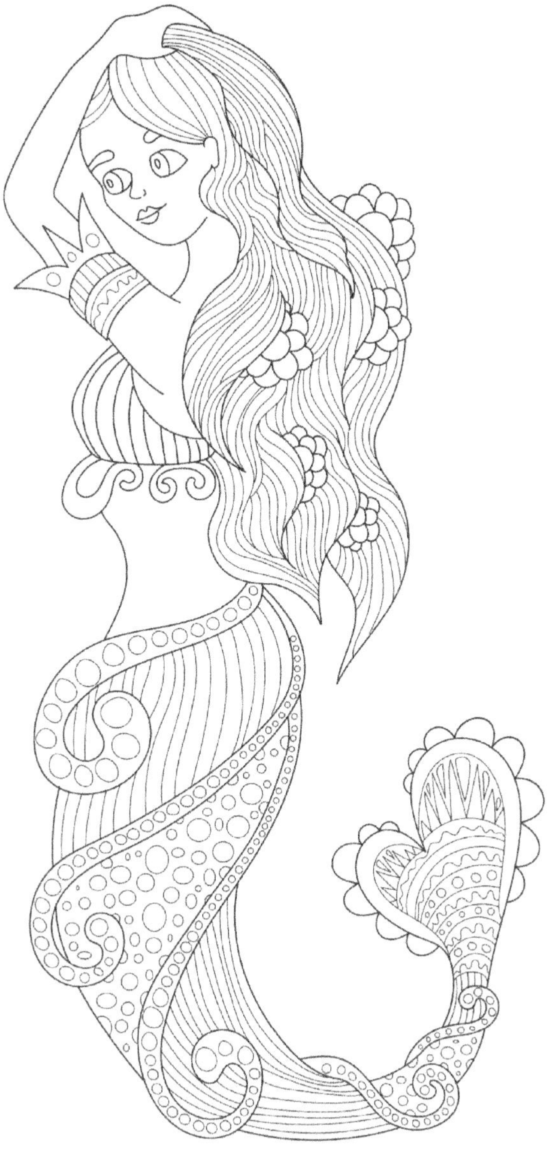

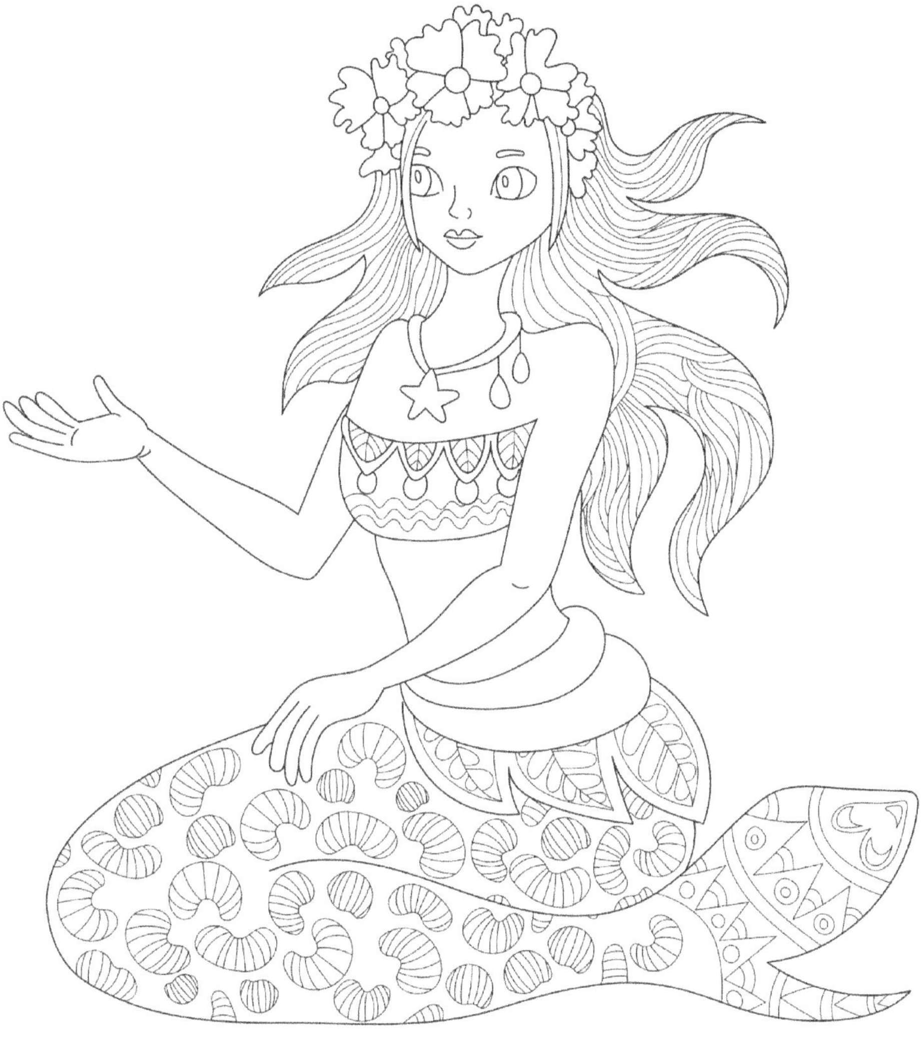

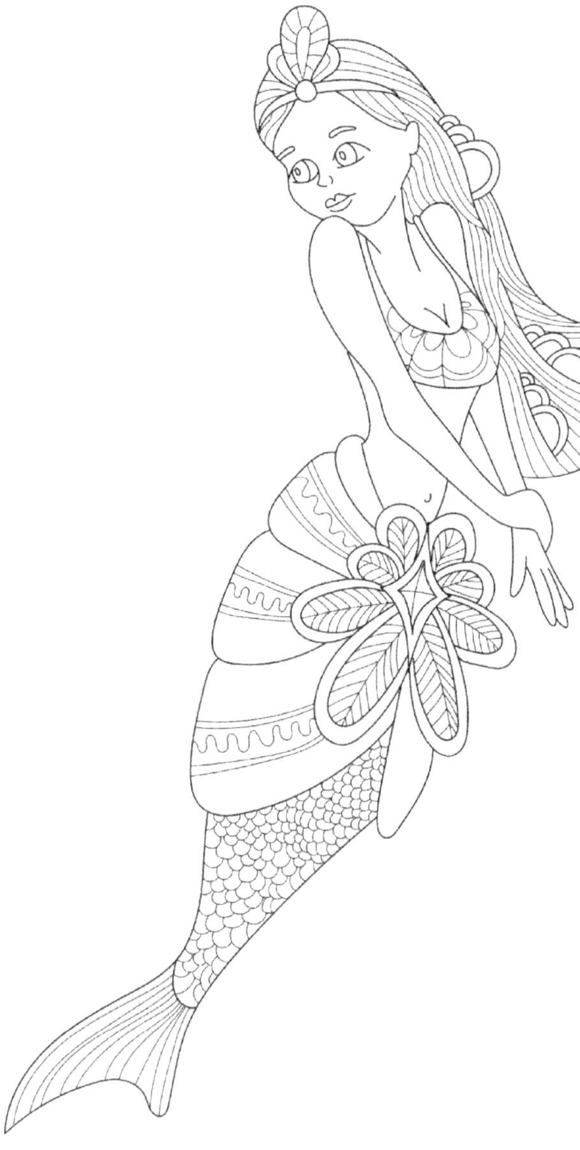

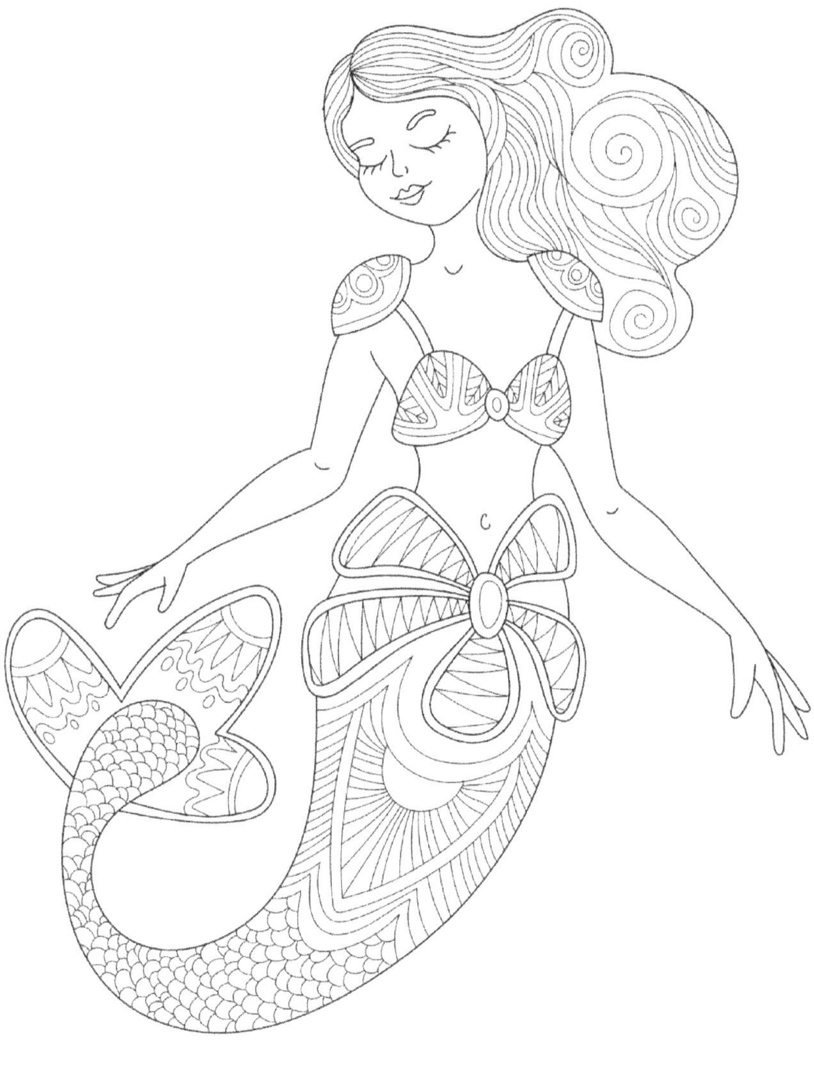

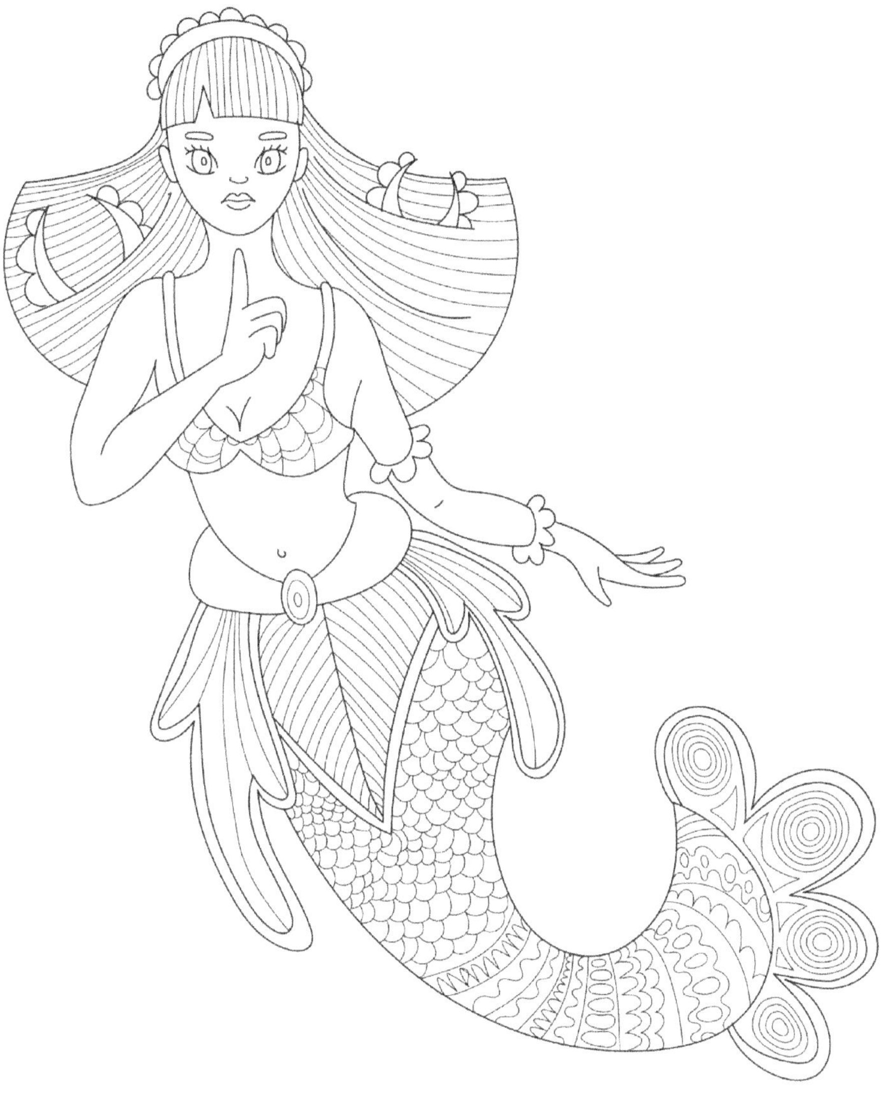

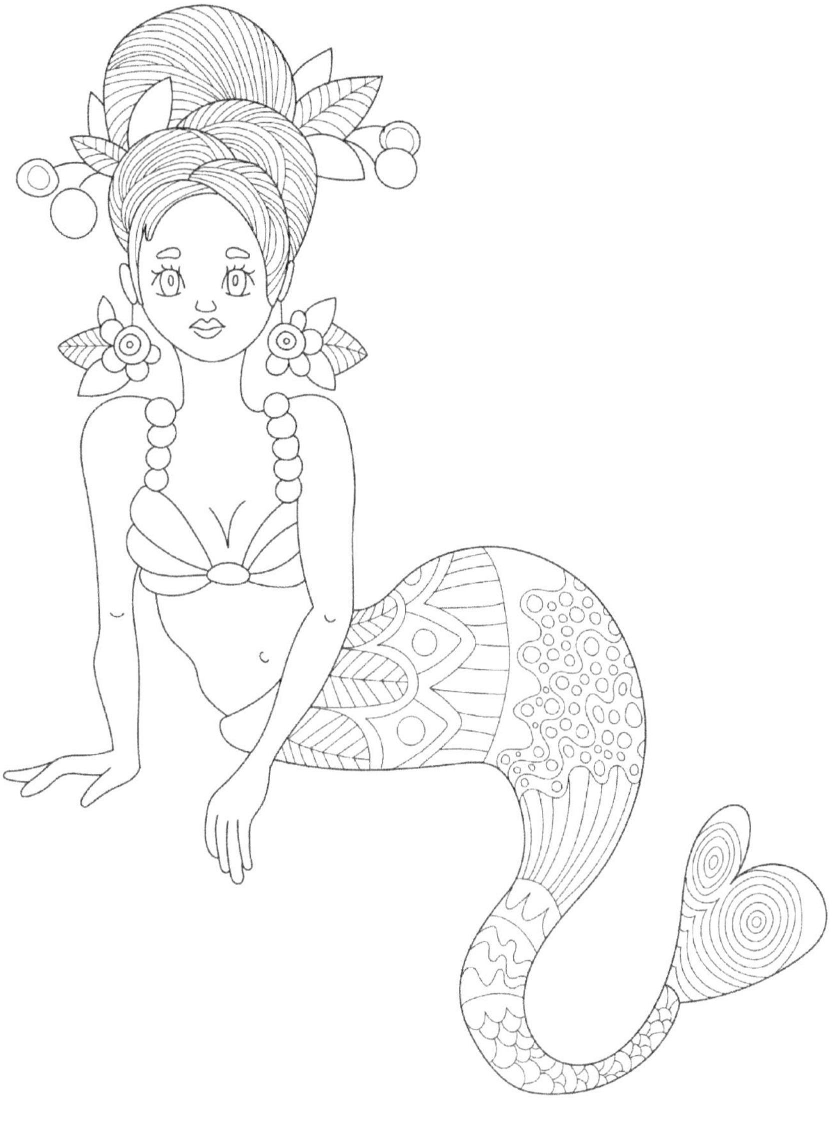

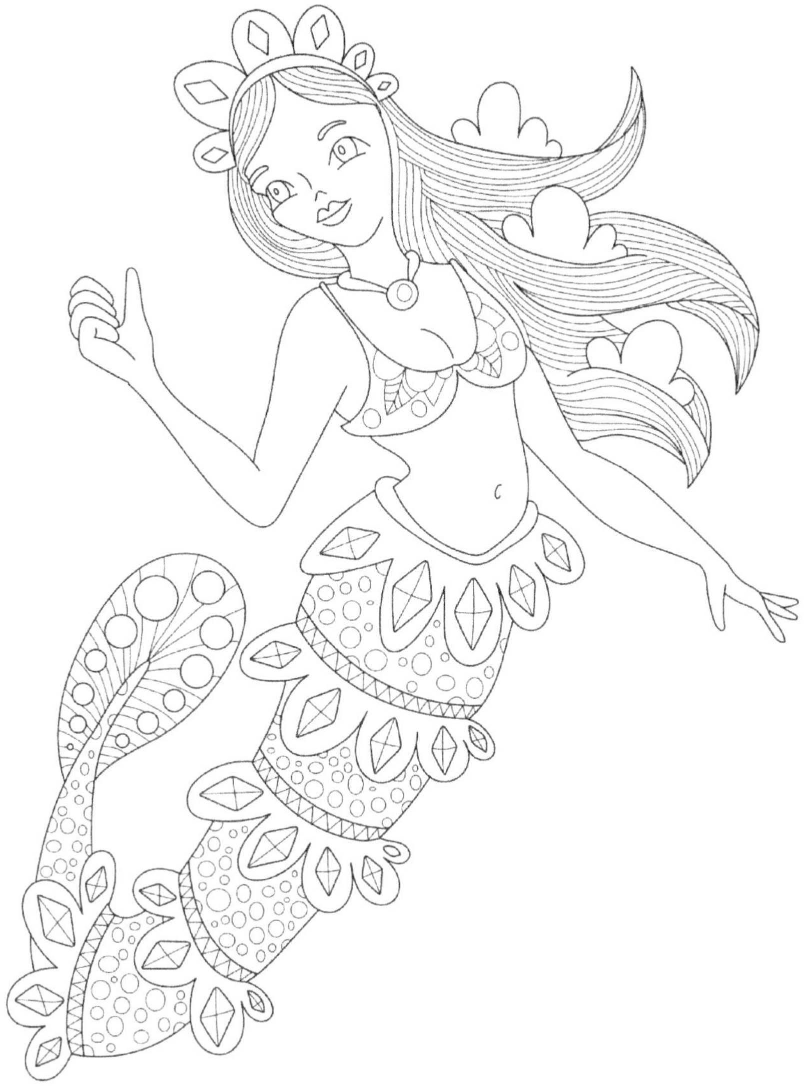

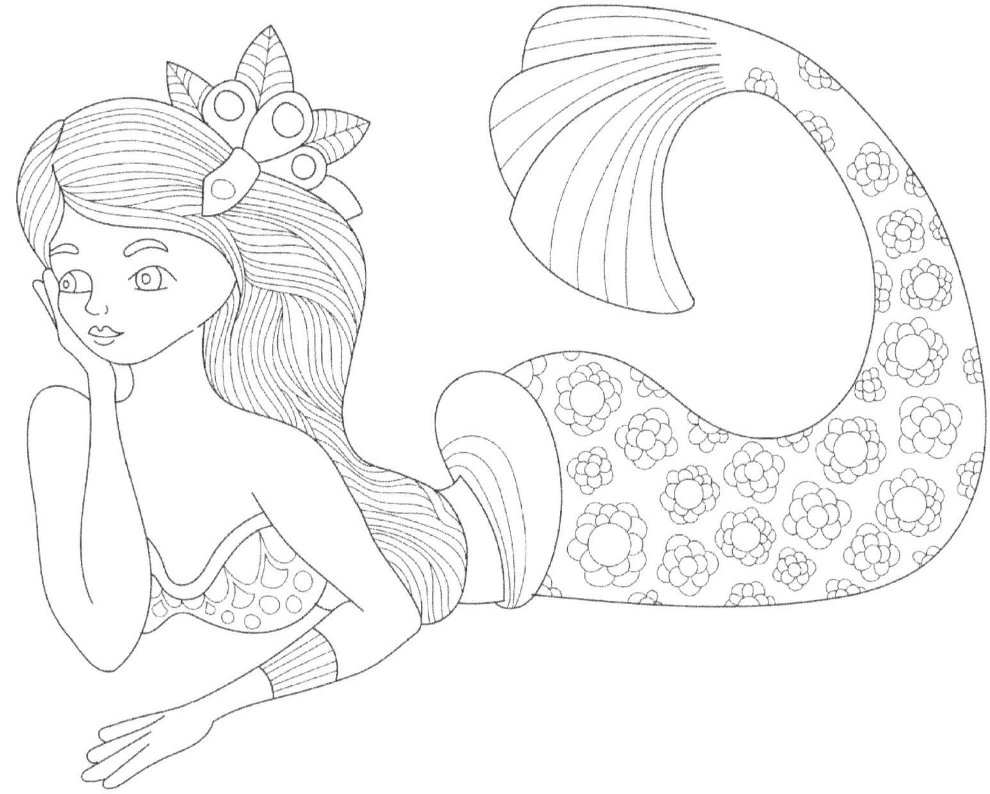

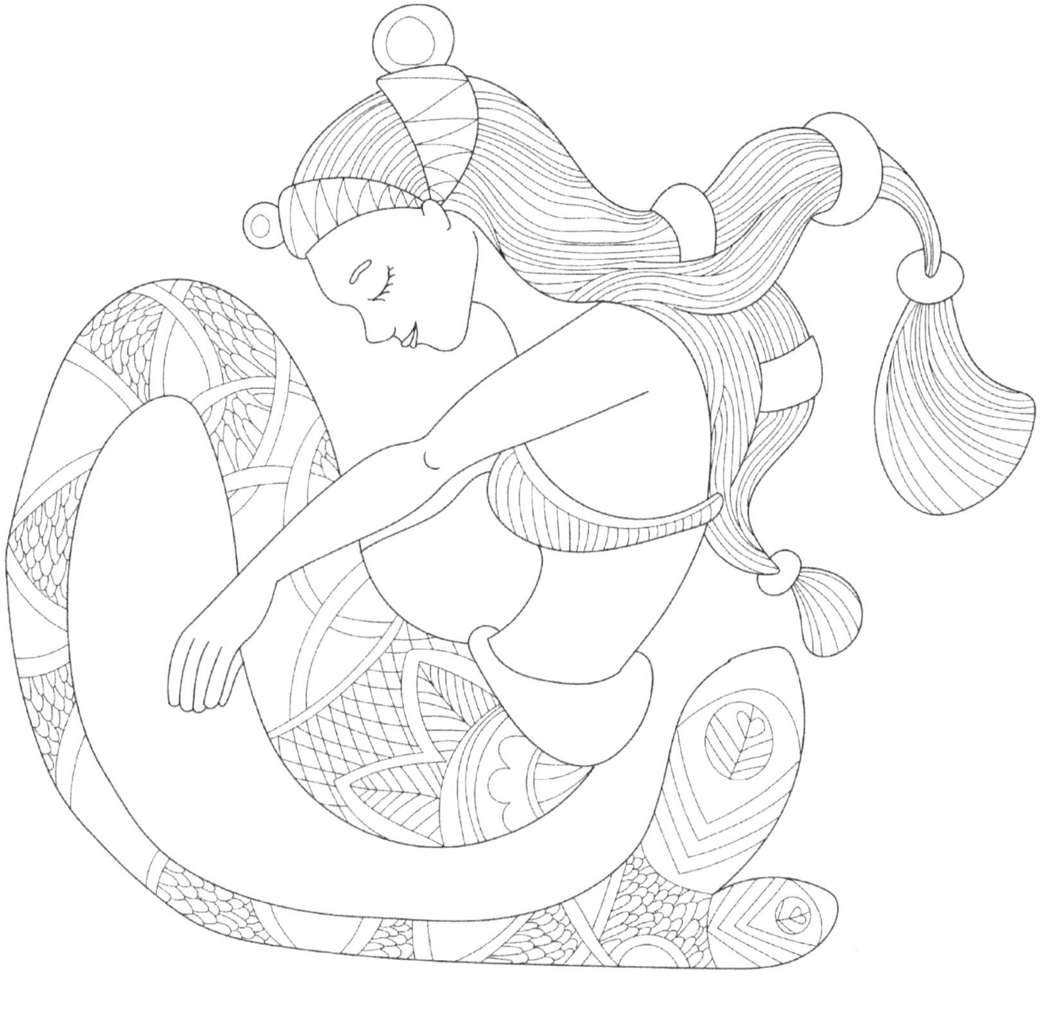

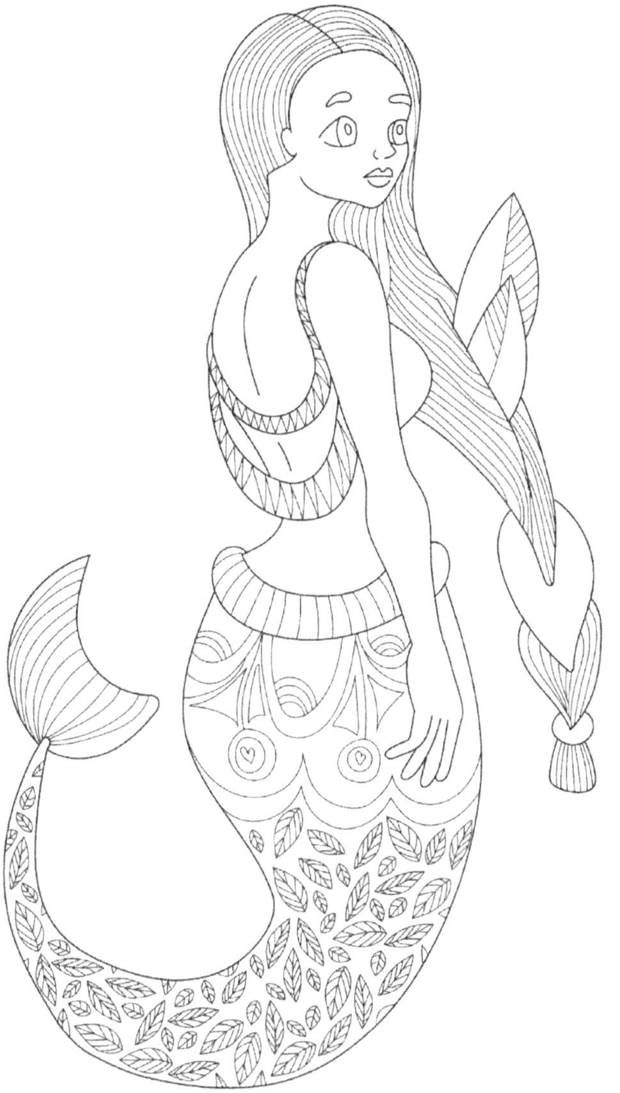

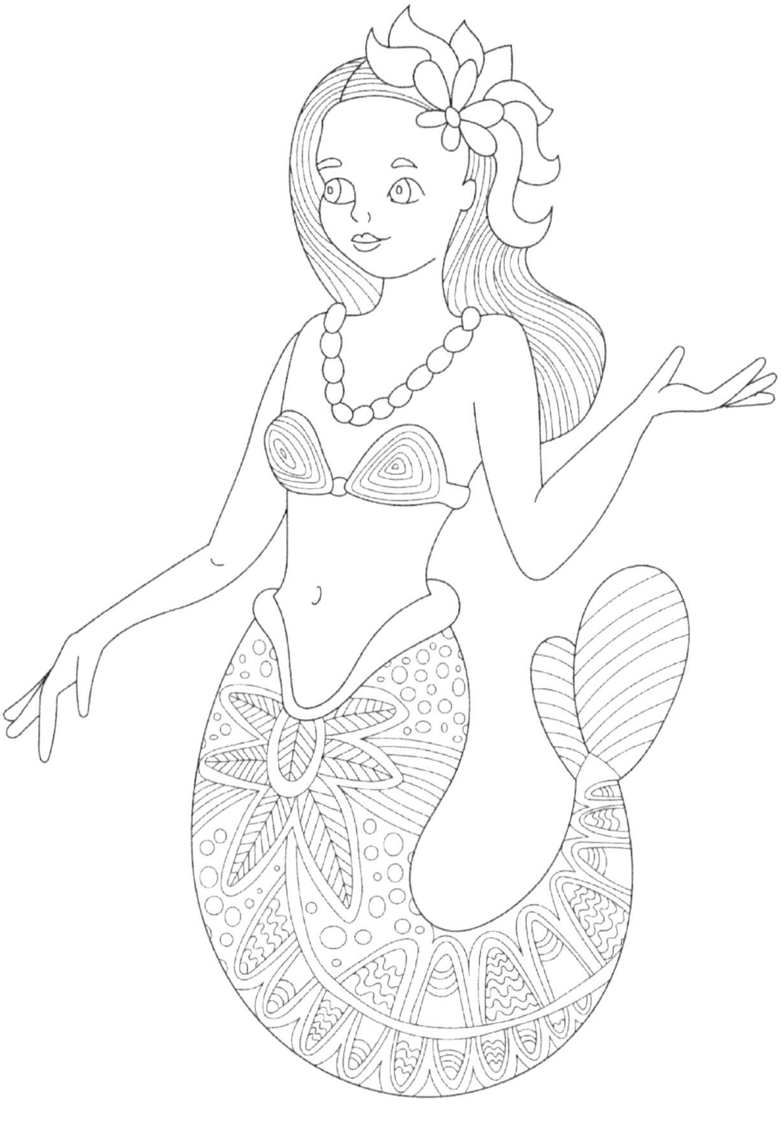

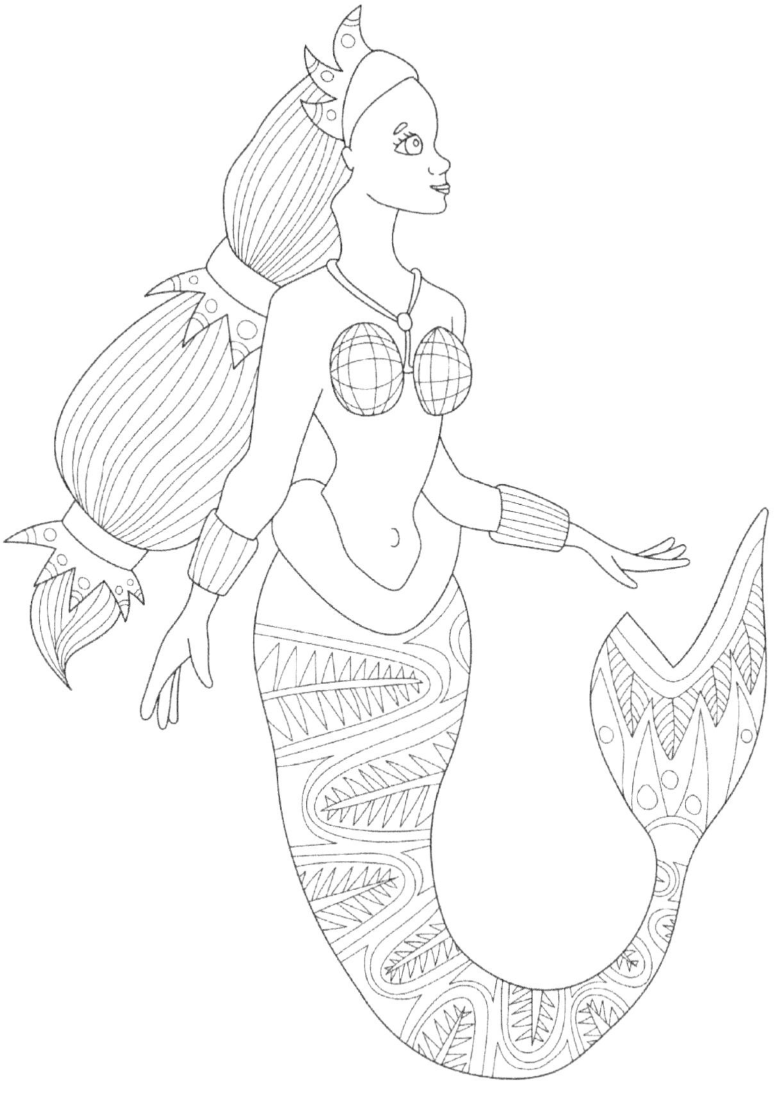

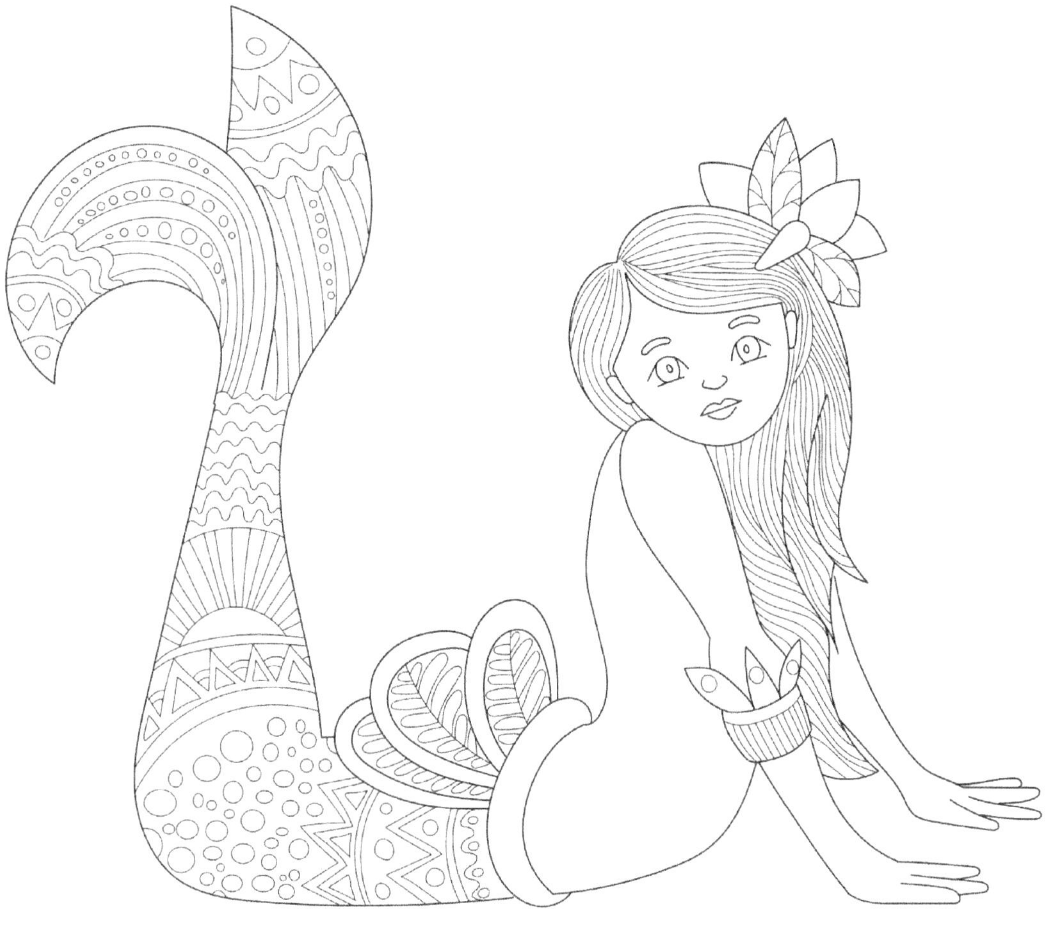

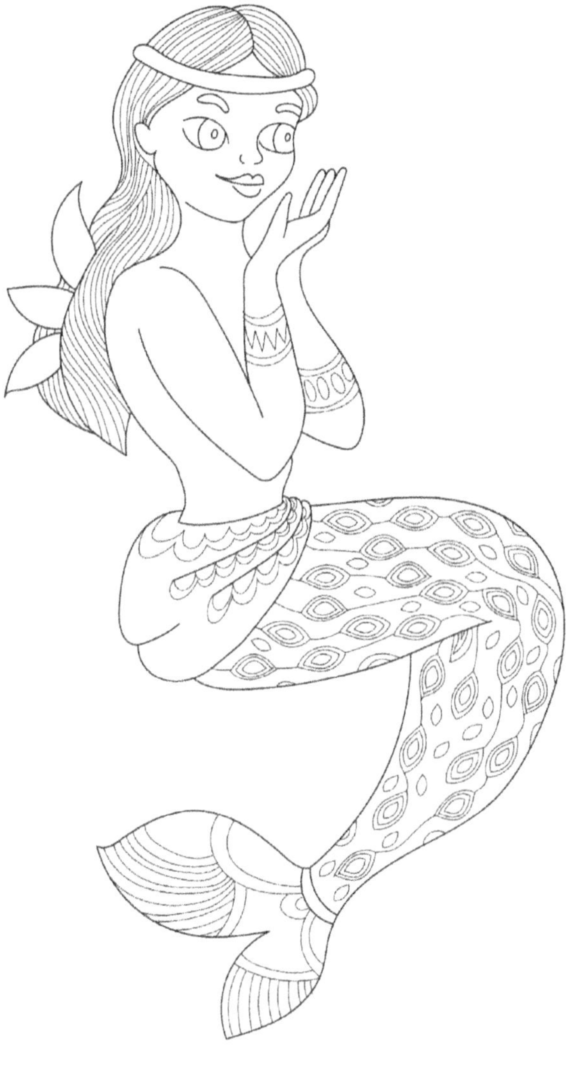

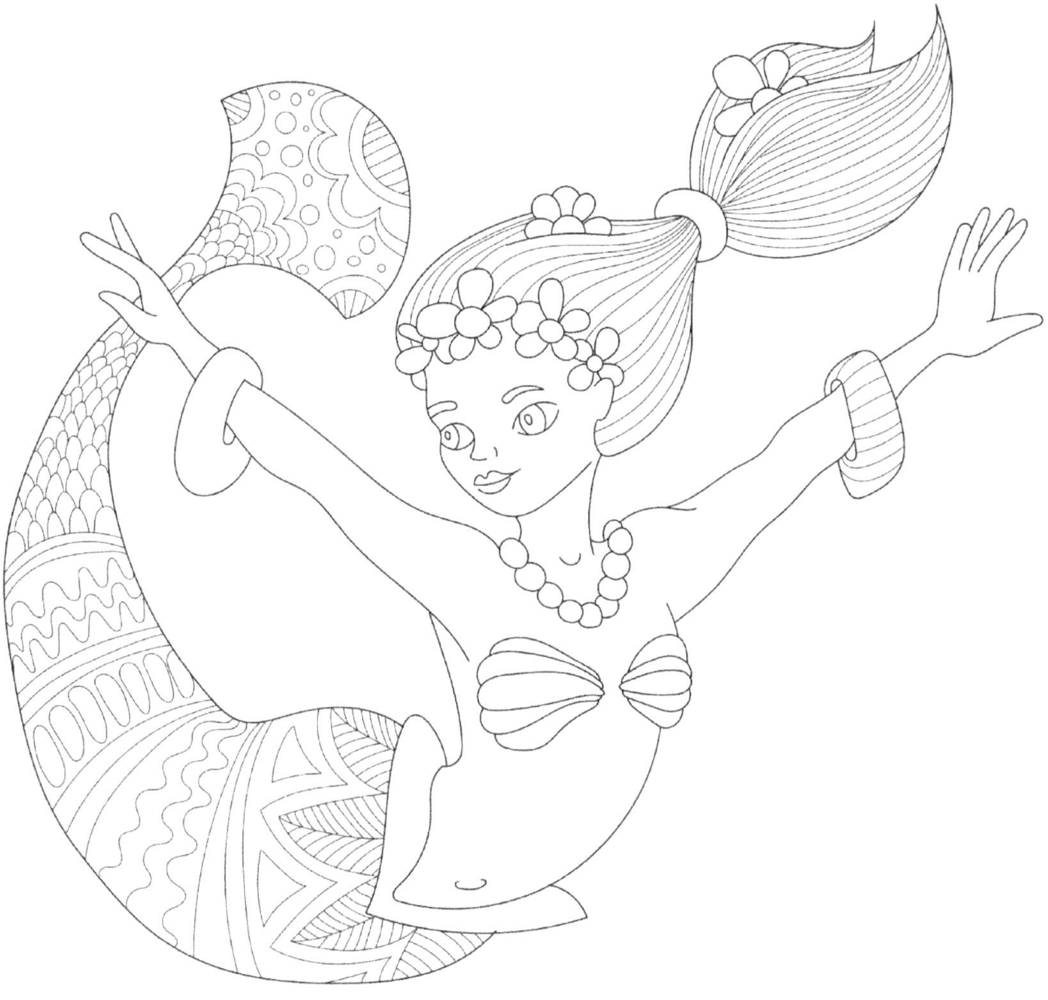

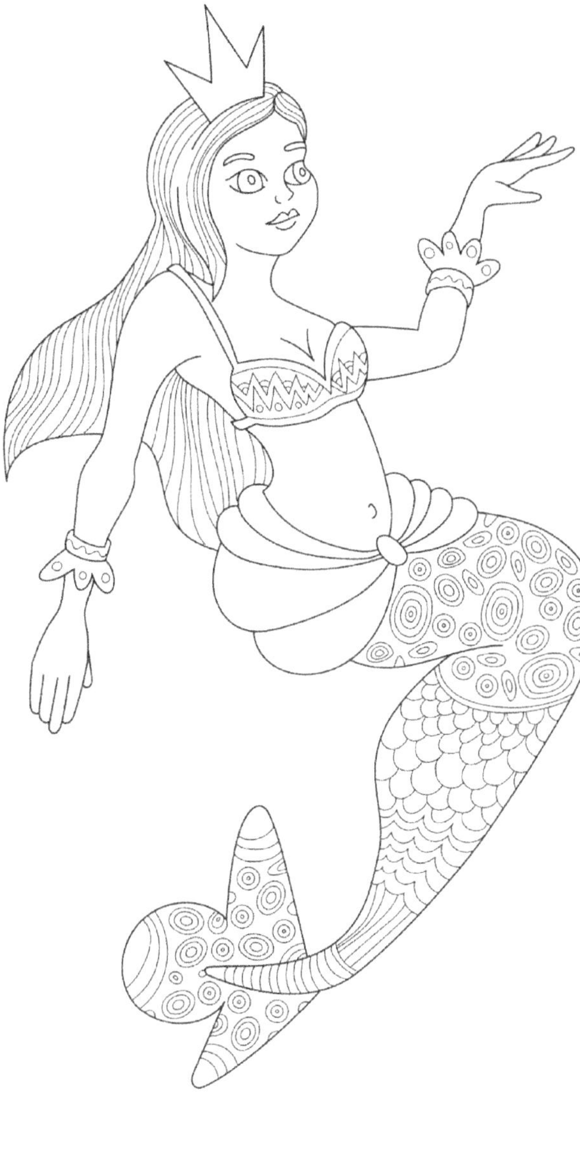

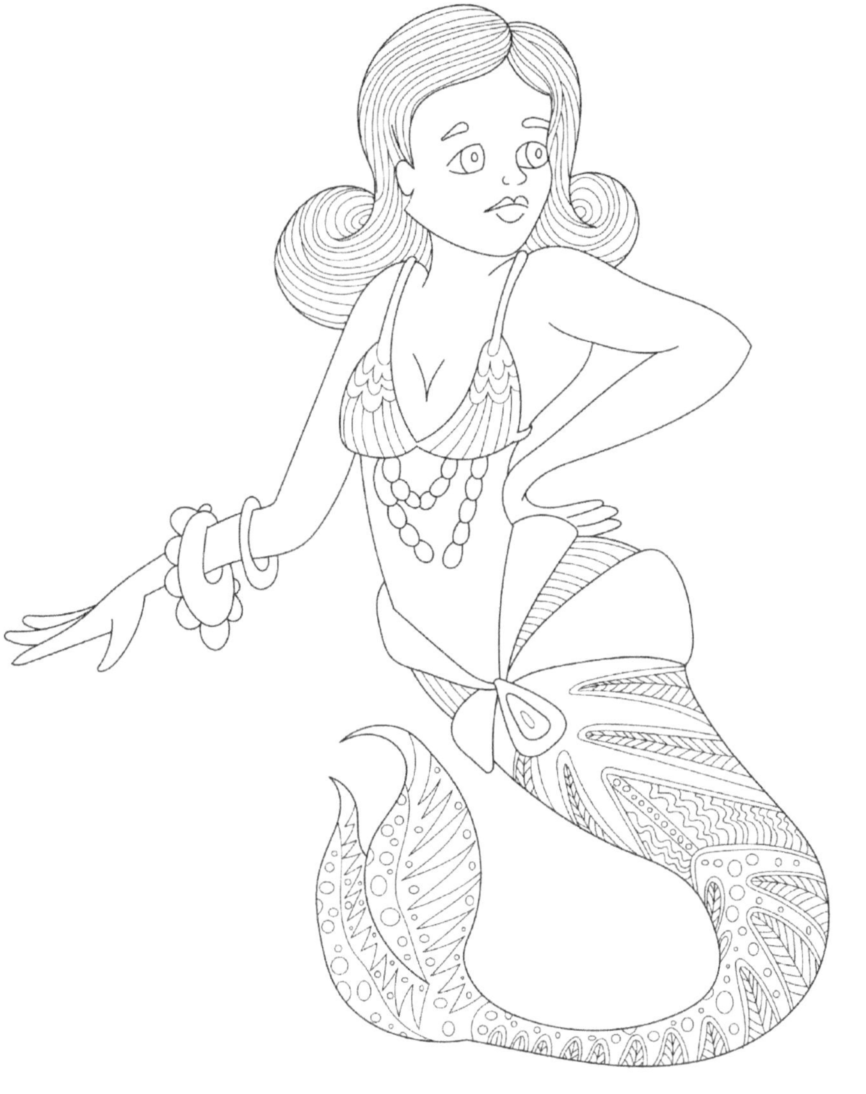

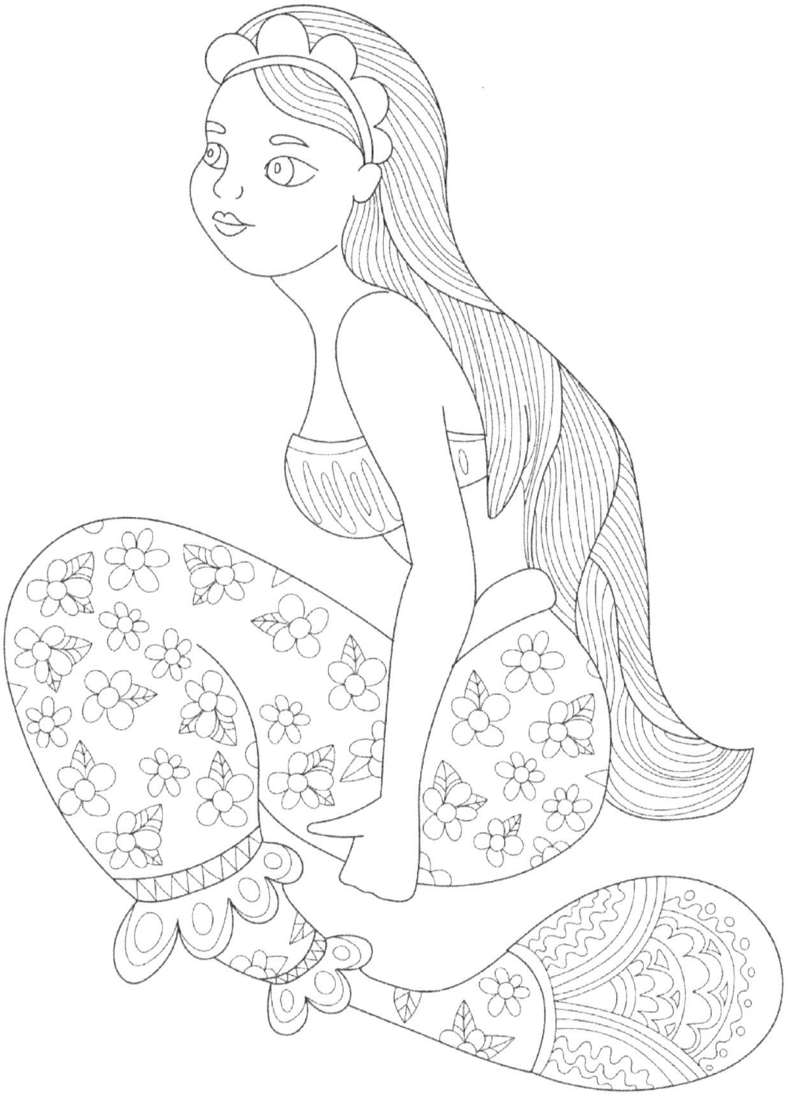

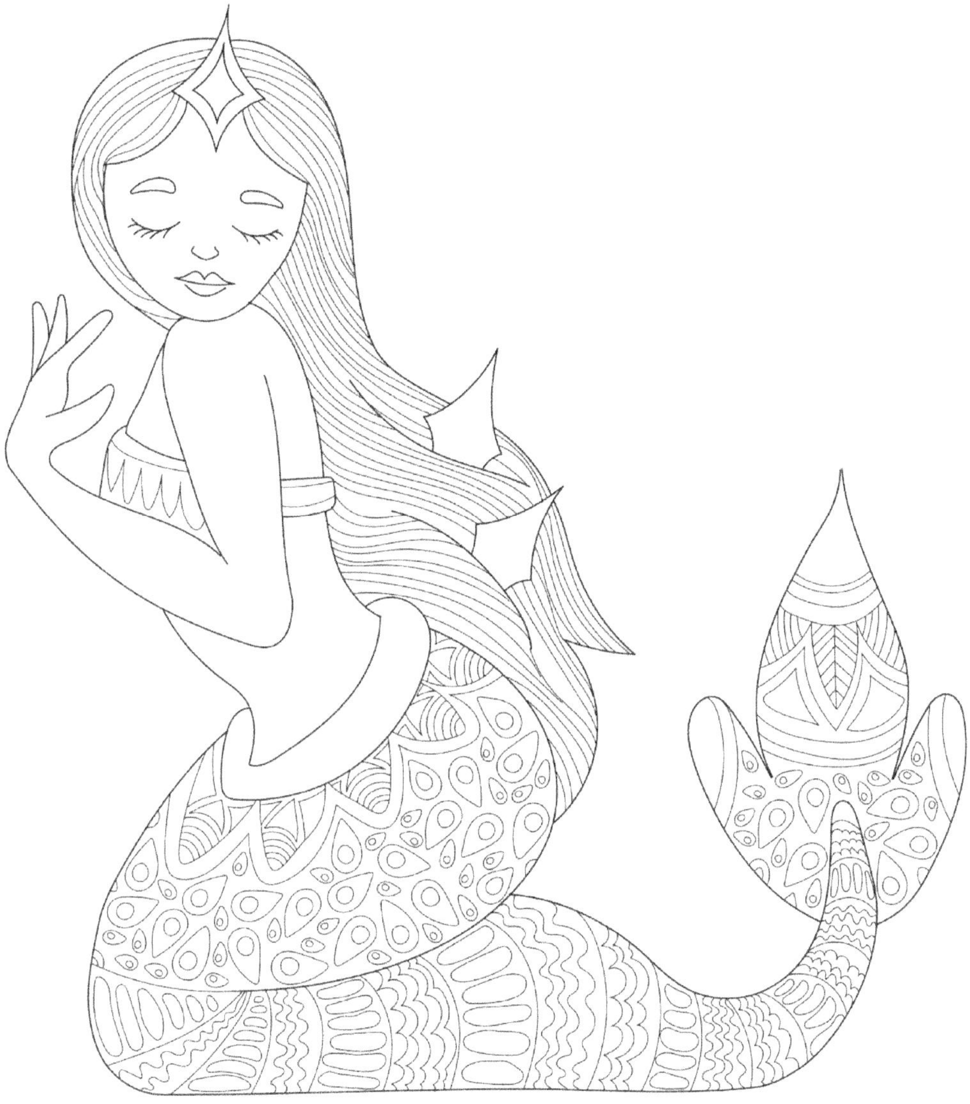

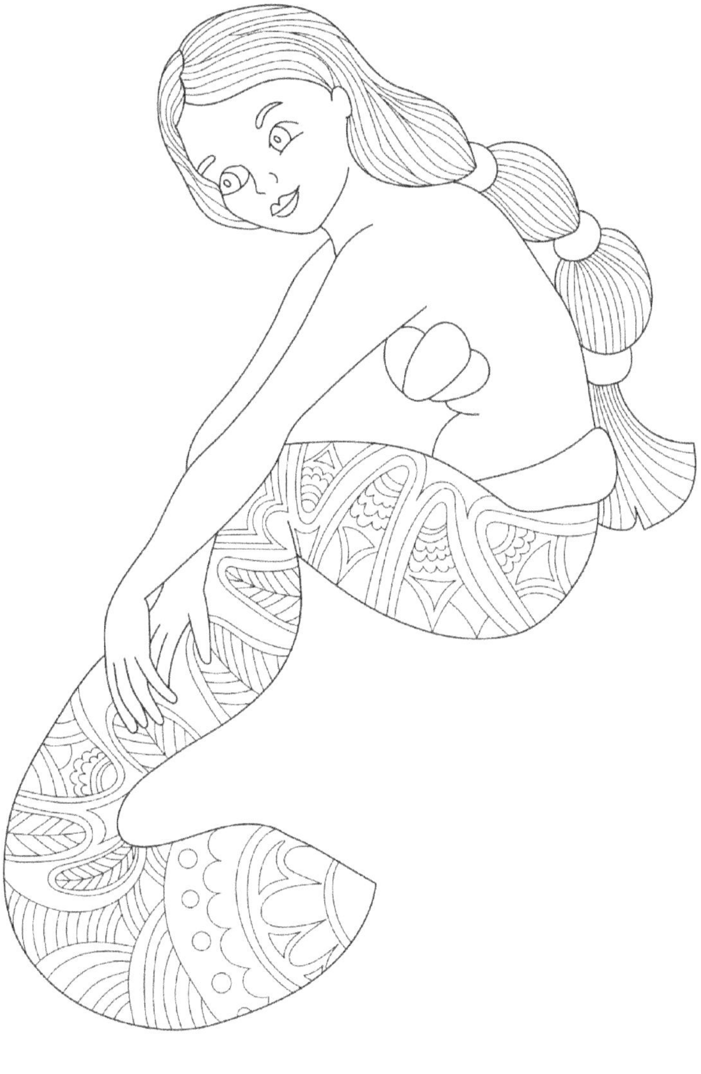

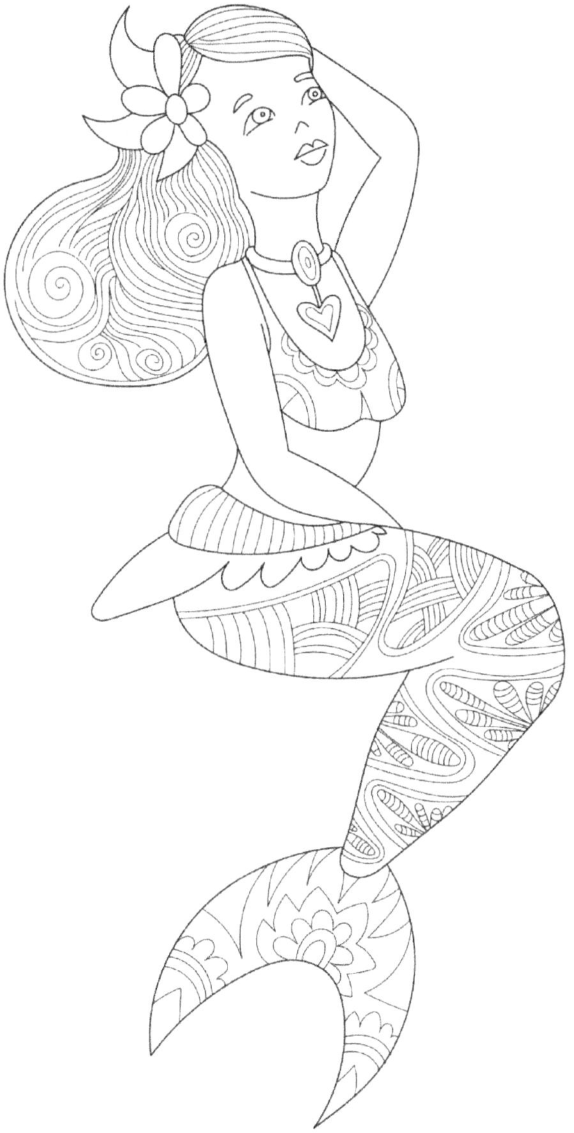

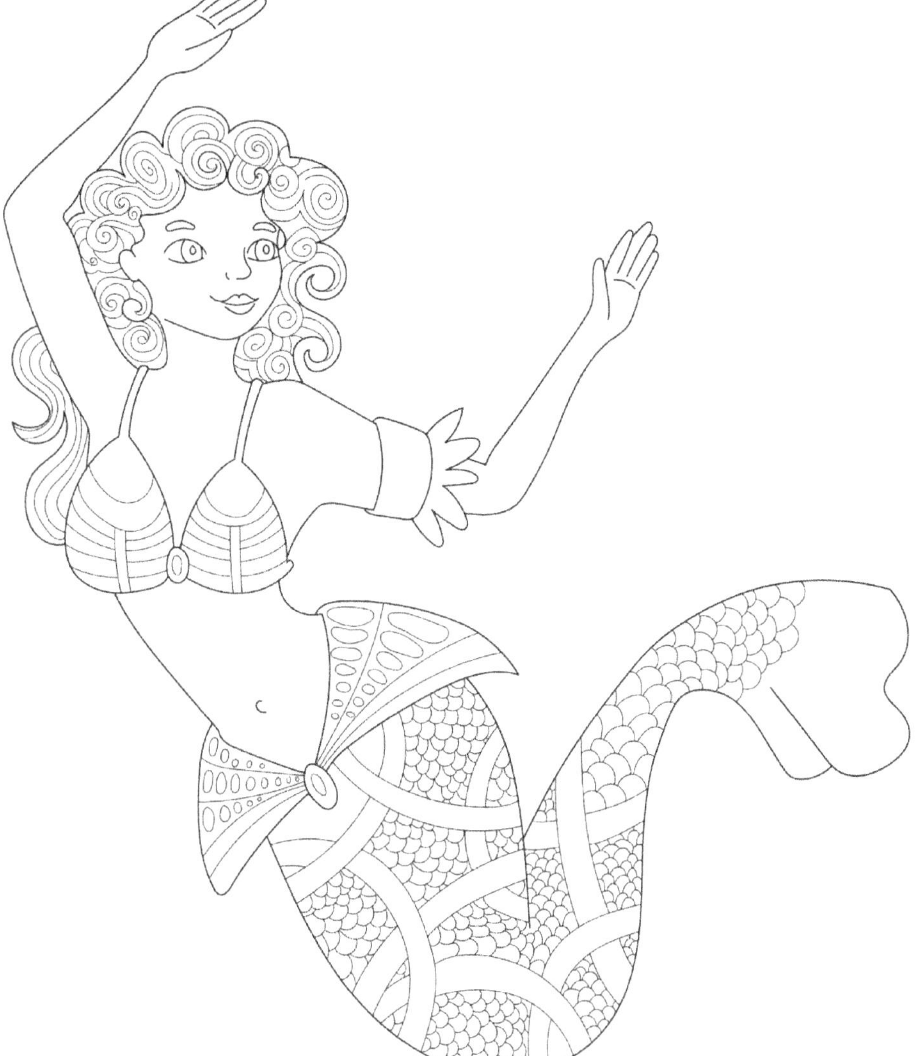

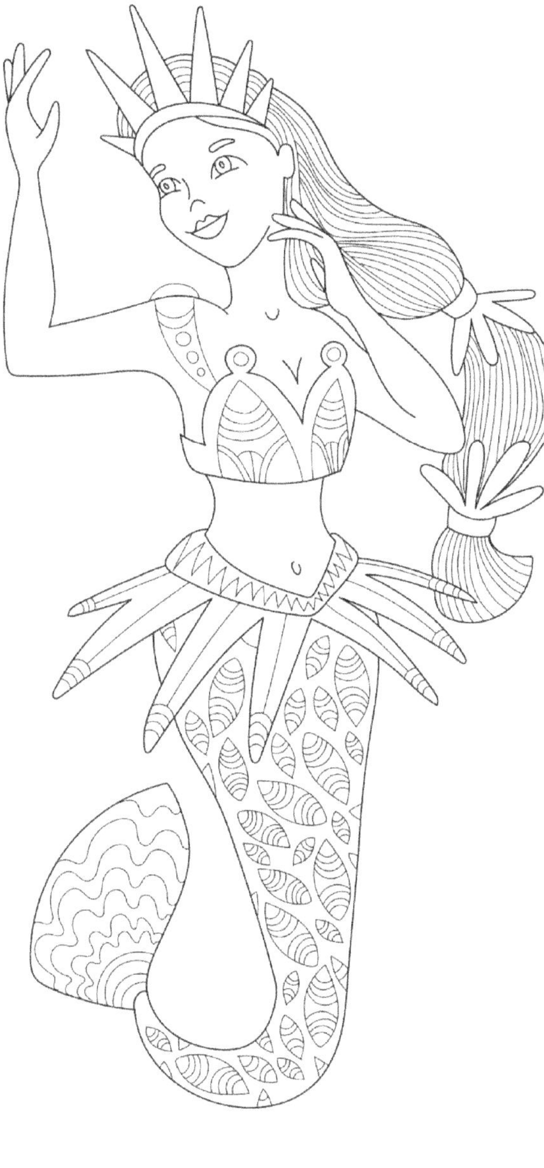

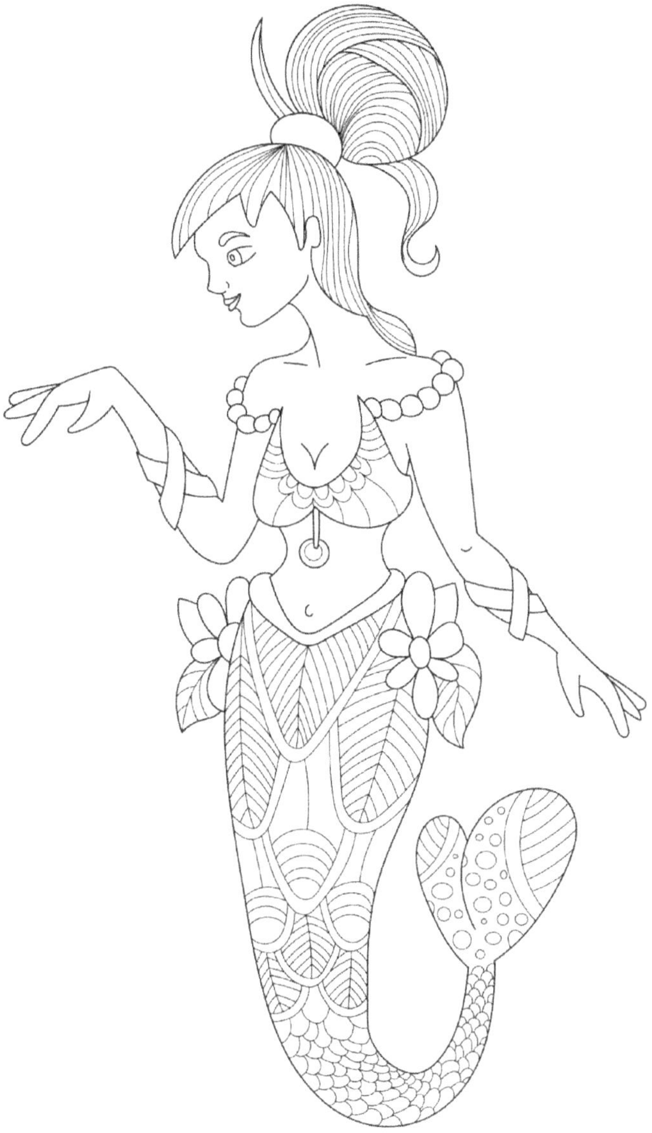

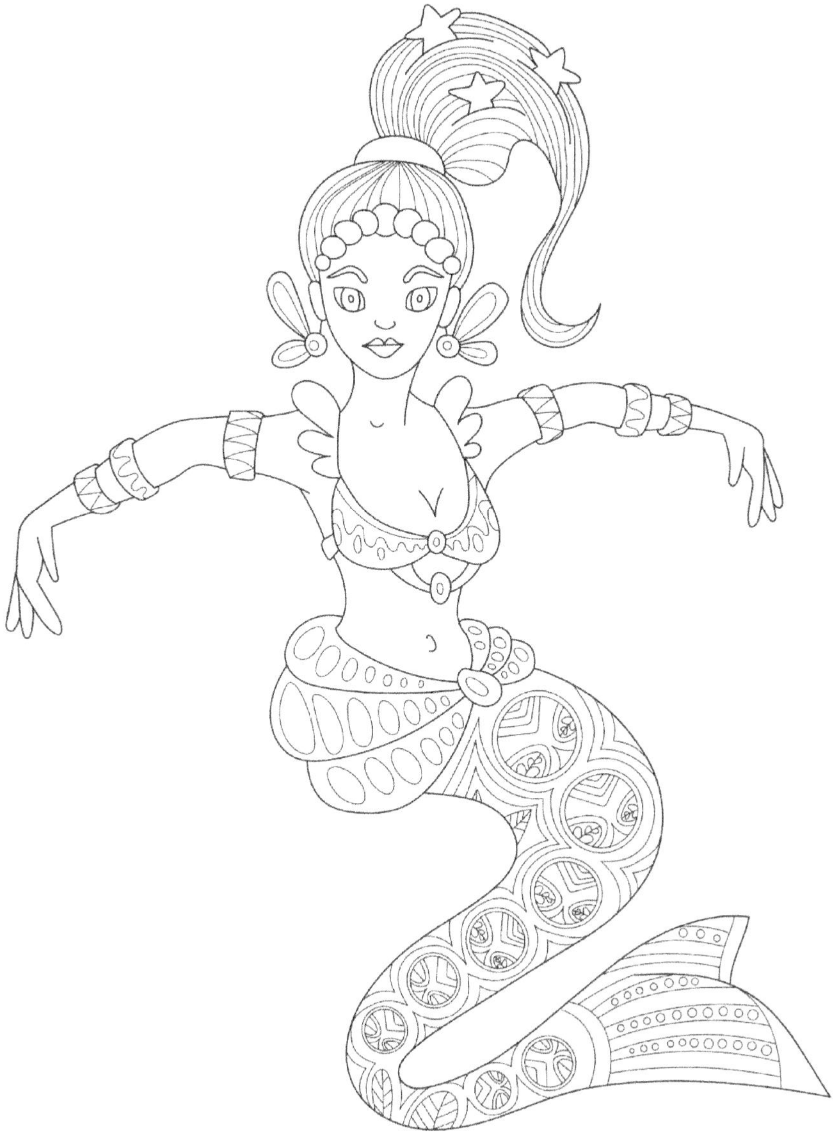

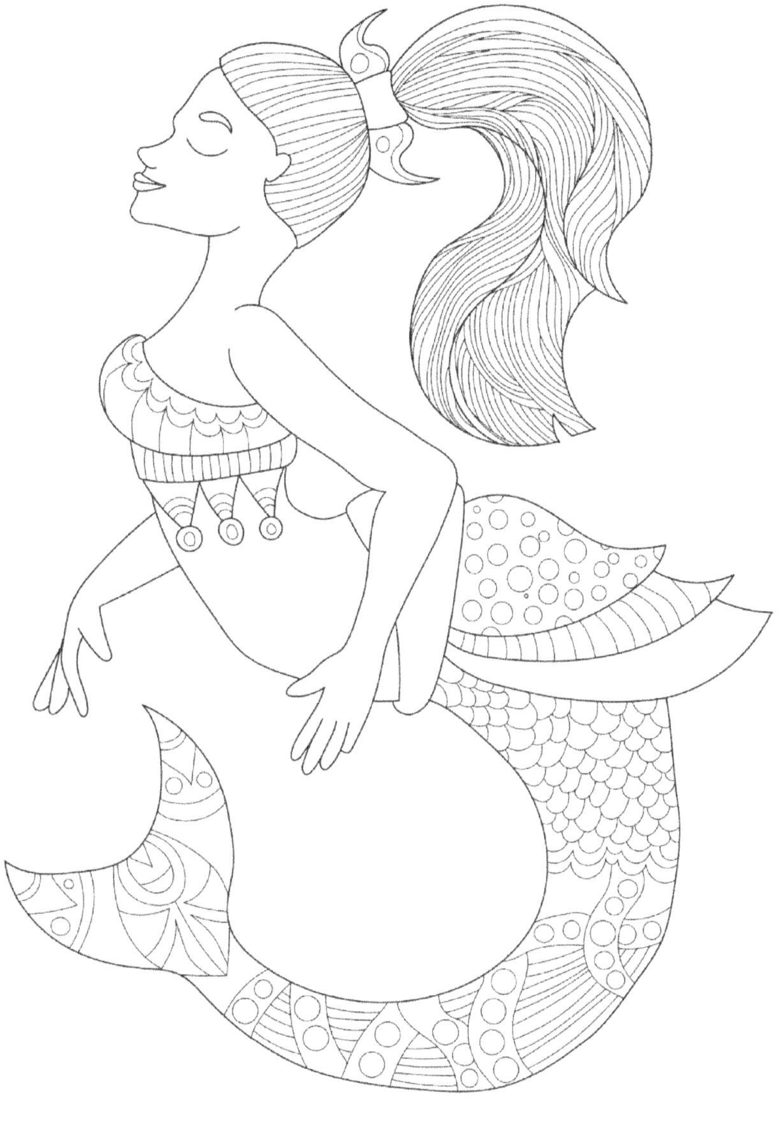

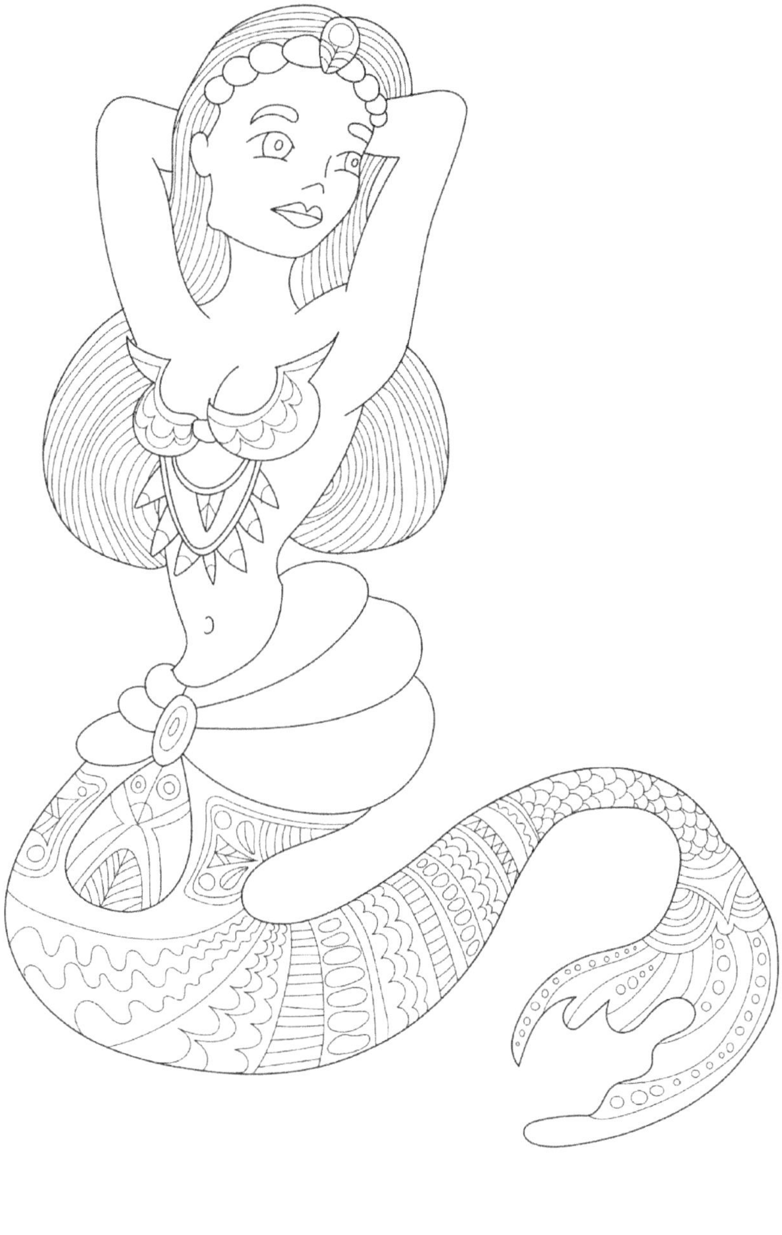

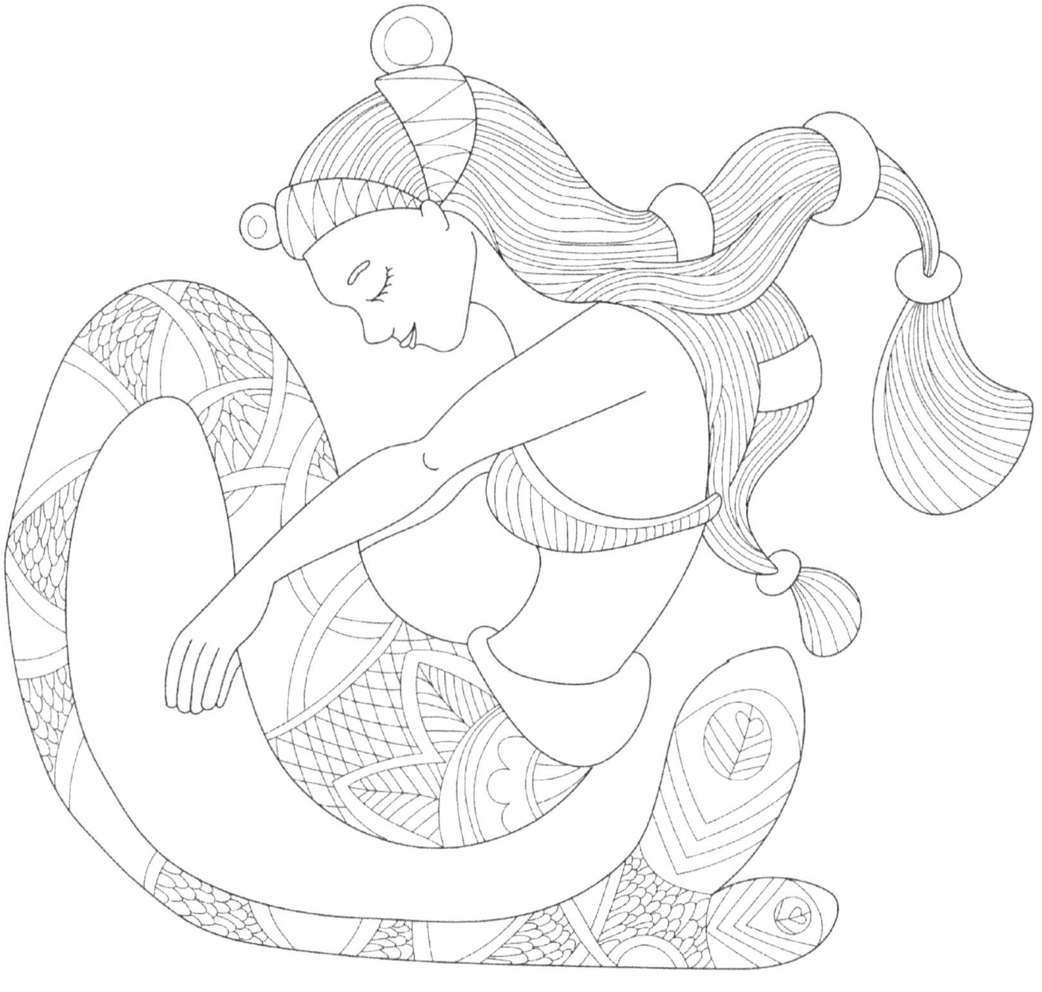

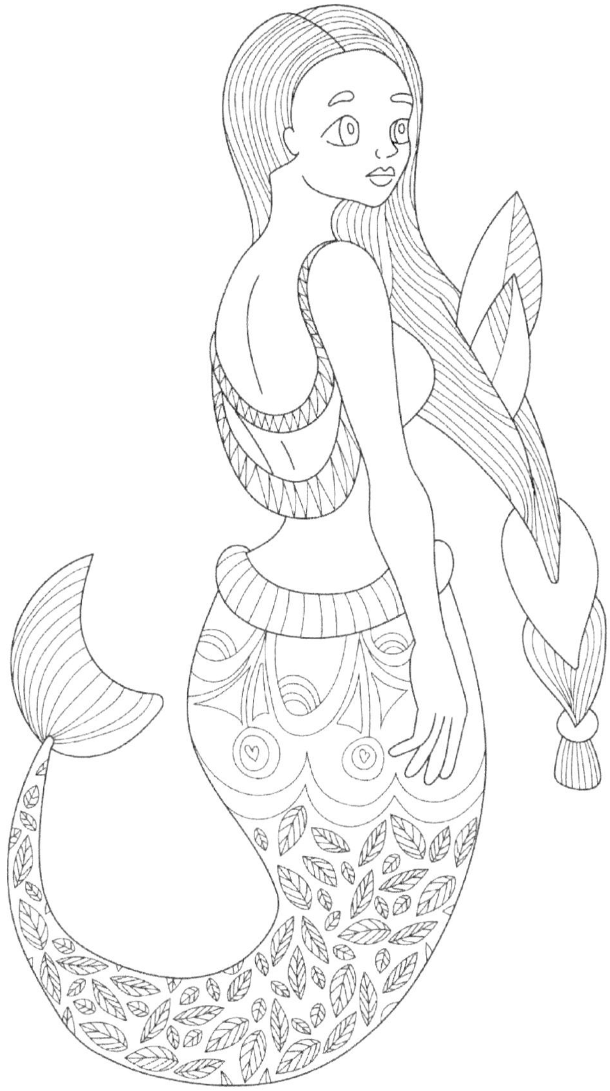

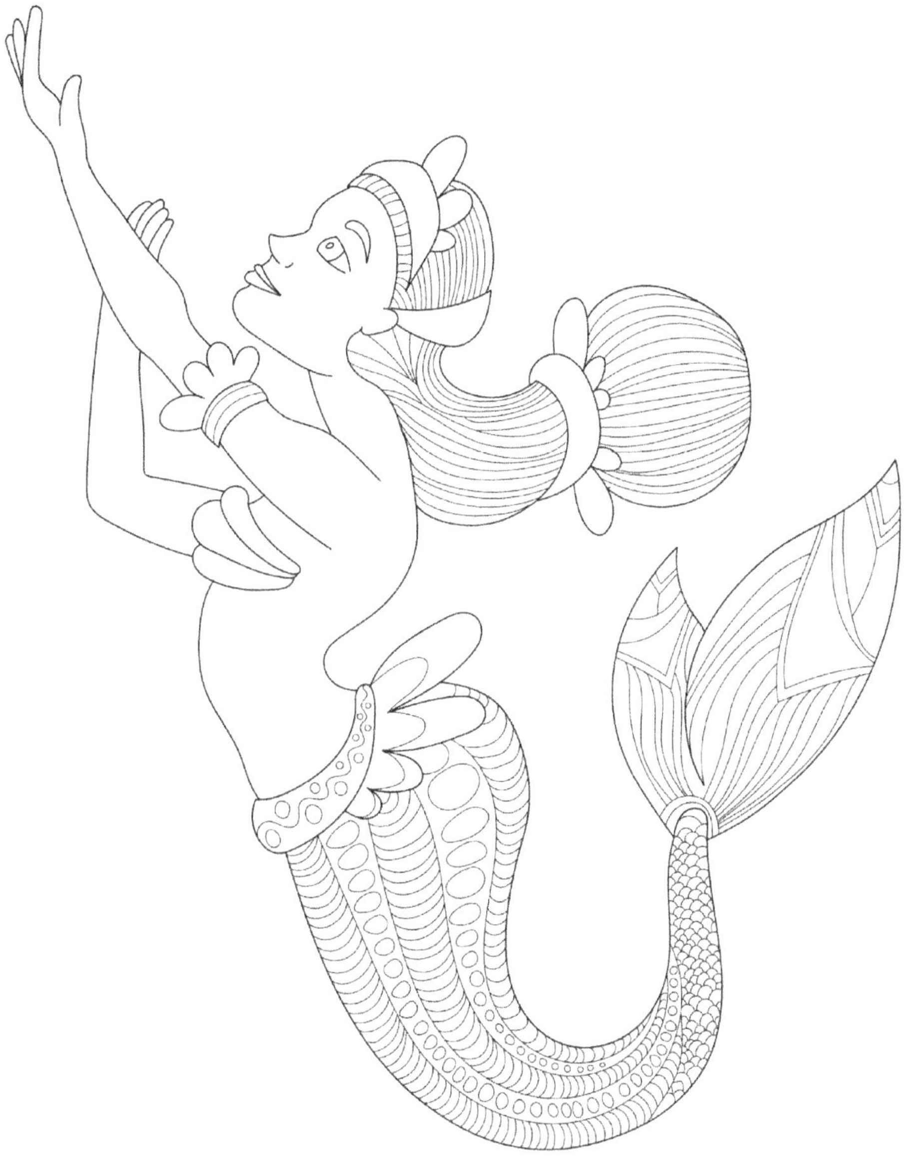

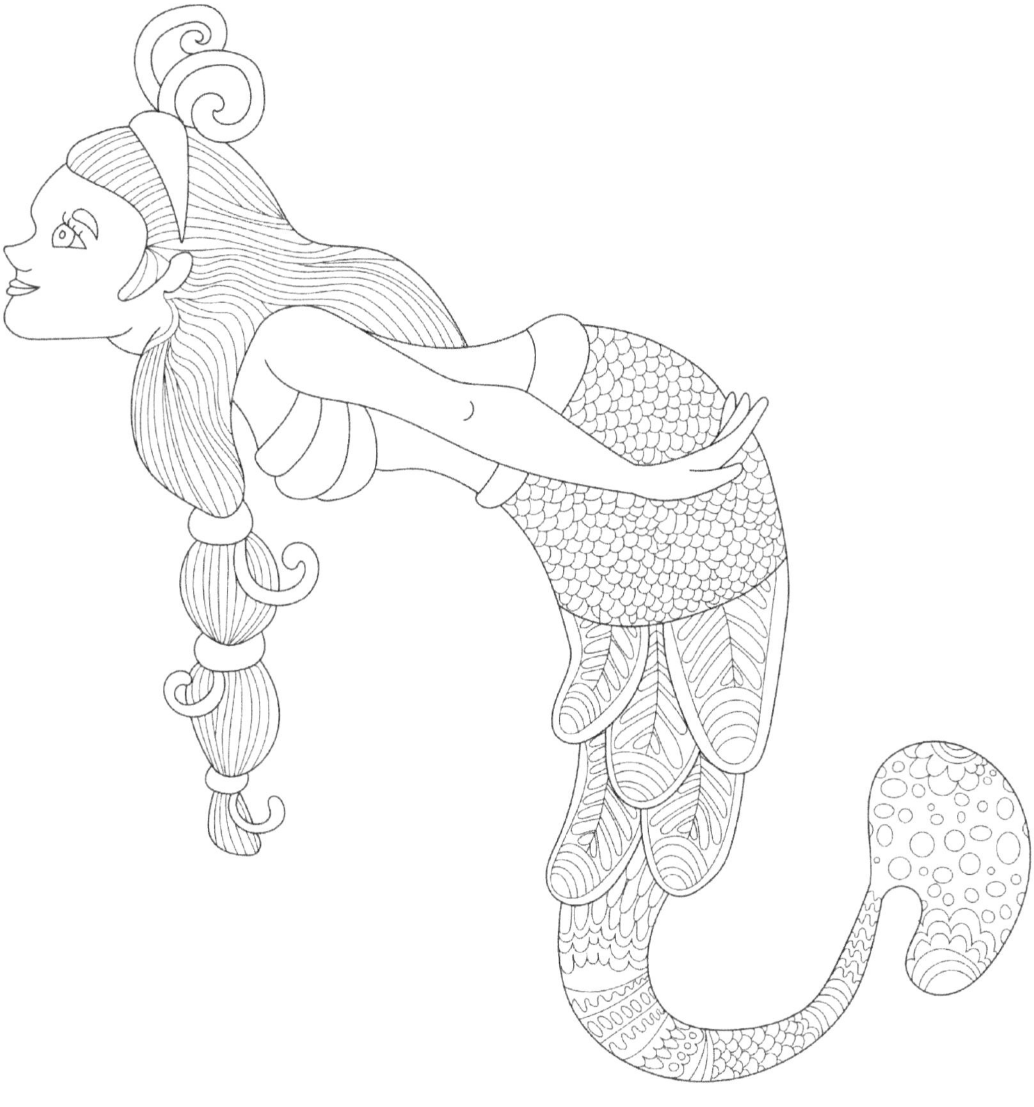

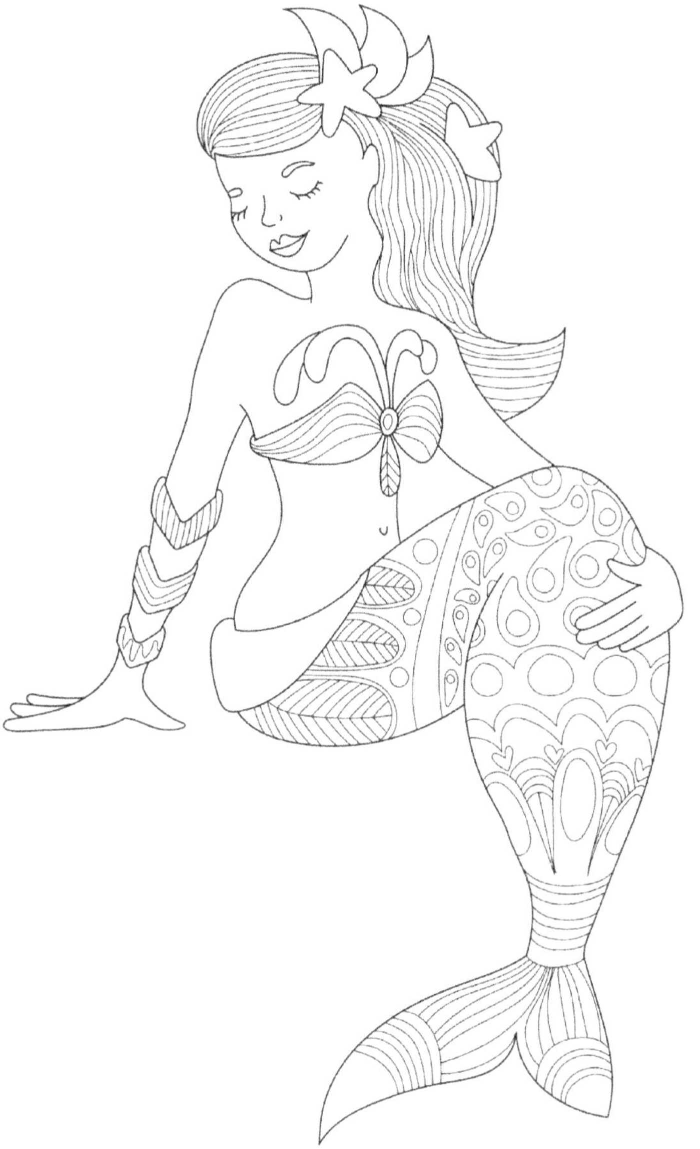

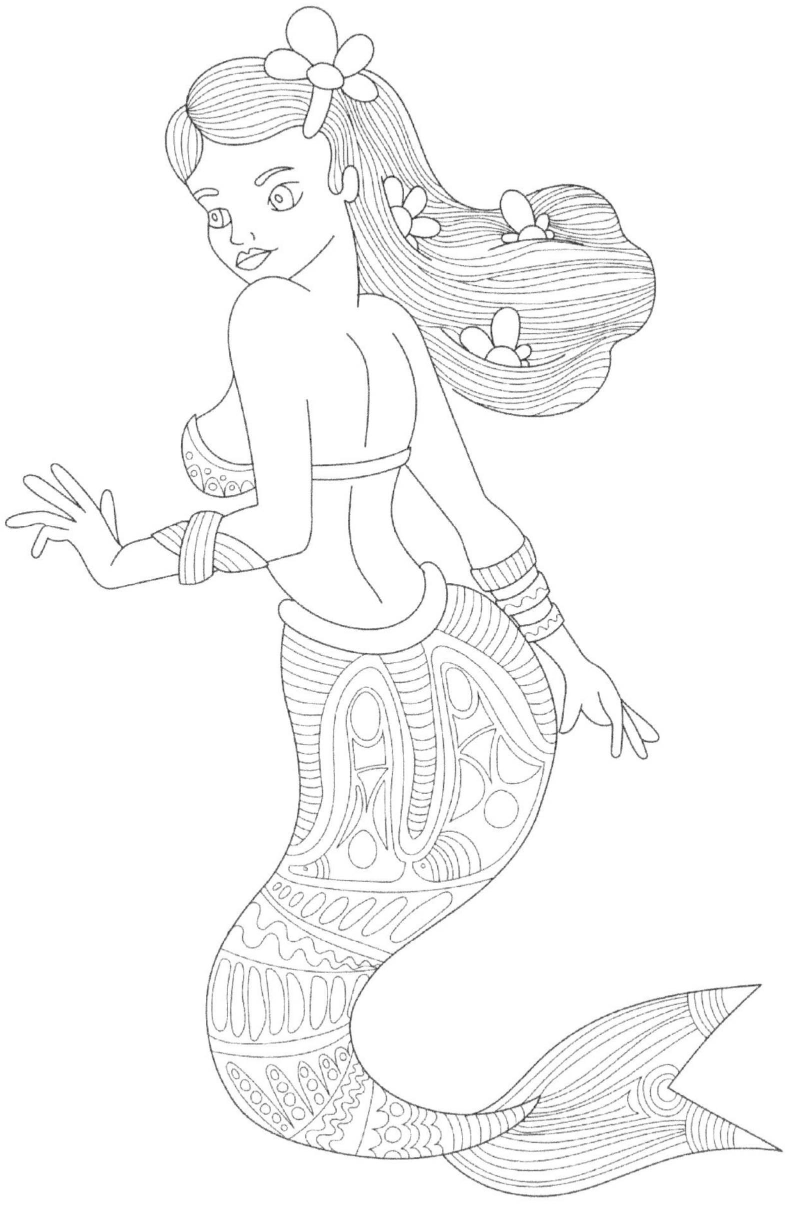

www.ingramcontent.com/pod-product-compliance
Lightning Source LLC
Chambersburg PA
CBHW080837220526
45467CB00008B/2305
9781706822011